THE YOUNG
MARTIAL ARTIST

THE YOUNG MARTIAL ARTIST

David Mitchell

PELHAM BOOKS

PELHAM BOOKS

Published by the Penguin Group
27 Wrights Lane, London W8 5TZ, England
Viking Penguin, a division of Penguin Books USA Inc, 375 Hudson Street, New York, NY
10014, USA

Penguin Books Australia Ltd, Ringwood, Victoria, Australia
Penguin Books Canada Ltd, 10 Alcorn Avenue, Suite 300, Toronto, Ontario, Canada
M4V 3B2
Penguin Books (NZ) Ltd, 182–190 Wairau Road, Auckland 10, New Zealand

Penguin Books Ltd, Registered Offices: Harmondsworth, Middlesex, England

First published 1992
Copyright © David Mitchell, 1992

Typeset in Linotron 11 on 13pt Clearface Regular by
Goodfellow & Egan Phototypesetting Ltd, Cambridge
Printed and bound in Great Britain by
Butler & Tanner Ltd, Frome

A CIP catalogue record for this book is available from the British Library.

ISBN 0 7207 1911 9

The moral right of the author has been asserted.

Photography throughout by Martin Sellars unless otherwise indicated.

The martial arts are potentially dangerous: the author, producers and pub-
lishers will accept no liability for damage or injuries resulting from the
performance of techniques described in this book.

Throughout the book, the young martial artist has been referred to as 'he'. This
is for simplicity only.

Contents

Acknowledgements   7

Introduction   9

Fitness & The Young Martial Artist   14

Fitness Games I   20

Fitness Games II   38

Basic Skills I   58

Basic Skills II   65

Basic Skills III   81

Getting Started   101

The Syllabus   105

Glossary   118

Index   128

Acknowledgements

Though I have taught martial arts for around twenty-five years, I am relatively new to coaching and have no more than a decade of experience to draw on. This means that some of the knowledge contained in this book comes from other sources and it gives me great pleasure to acknowledge them here:

Dr. J.C. Canney is the mainstay of medical advice to the martial arts community in Britain, and to karate worldwide. Jim has done much to sweep aside the mysteries surrounding matters medical and render them comprehensible to the coach.

Tony Gummerson is a lecturer in Sports Science at the University of York. Before Tony was encouraged to turn his attention towards the martial arts, the latter knew virtually nothing about coaching. Tony's uncompromising approach to practical coaching has sat many a know-it-all back on his heels (me for one!).

Martin Lee is head of the Institute For The Study of Children In Sport, Bedford. His lectures on child psychology explain why so many children join – and as quickly leave – martial art clubs.

John White is a National Coach of the British Amateur Gymnastics Association, with responsibility for recreational gymnastics. John has shed light on such areas as technique progression, where previously the darkness of ignorance prevailed.

Robert Clark, the National Coach of the British Jiu Jitsu Association, provided two coaches who specialise in training young students and he also kindly loaned us some safety mats.

I would like to turn now to the models I used for this book. The James family of Wolverhampton – Jennie (the eldest), Darren and Naomi study karate with Eddie Hines of the Higashi Karate Kai. Jennie has been training for 18 months and is a 5th kyu. She also enjoys trampolining, swimming, canoeing and sailing. Darren has been training for 18 months and is also a 5th kyu. He shares the same interests as Jennie except that he also plays football. Naomi has been training for 2 months and enjoys the same activities as her siblings.

David and Steven Higginbotham both come from Southport, Merseyside. David is the elder and he has been training for three years. His teacher is Alan Campbell of the British Jiu Jitsu Association. David is a keen swimmer (he is a member of Southport swimming club and has represented his county), and enjoys badminton and football. Steven has also been training for three years and holds brown belt grade. Steven shares his brother's interests and has been a Cub since the age of eight.

Carl Booth is also from Southport and trains with David and Steven. He has been training for three years and is a brown belt. Carl enjoys swimming and football and is a Cub too.

It is said that young people and animals are difficult to work with. Until I do a book on animals in the martial arts, I'll have to reserve judgement; but I can tell you that I've never enjoyed working with anyone – from international coaches downwards – so much as I did with Jennie, Darren, Naomi, David, Steve and Carl.

David Mitchell,
Penrith,
July 1989.

Introduction

More and more children are joining martial arts classes. I don't know why this should be but I can offer an opinion. Before doing so, however, I would point out that exactly the same thing happened in judo some twenty years ago. It used to be that judo was very much an adult's pastime. Its image was that of a mysterious and dangerous activity, used variously by inscrutable Chinese (sic) detectives such as Mr. Moto and Charlie Chan's 'Number One Son'. Later its image changed and it came to be regarded as a wholesome pastime which made youngsters tough. Who knows, perhaps the demise of the Saturday morning children's matinees turned them out of the cinemas and into the training halls!

Nowadays, karate, taekwondo and, to a lesser extent, kung fu have all but lost their menacing image and the black belt is now an unremarked member of society. Whether there is any connection or not, these martial arts are now as well attended by children as judo classes. In fact a recent survey by a member of the Martial Arts Commission revealed that sixty per cent of the entire membership is now below the age of sixteen! I have it on good authority that in ten years' time, that figure will have risen to around seventy-five per cent.

This book will, I hope, make it perfectly clear that if coaches expect to keep young students longer than a few weeks, then they will have to pull their fingers out and develop an appropriate form of training. Development will occur slowly in response to the twin pressures of competition and the ever-increasing threat of litigation for negligence. One of the directions that development will take is in the formulation of a martial arts syllabus for the below-twelves. Whether there is enough scope within individual martial arts or whether a general syllabus develops are matters of conjecture. Whatever happens, governing bodies of martial arts will not be able to go on indefinitely teaching an adult syllabus to non-adults.

The Coach's Responsibilities

The term 'duty of care' is something the coach needs to know about. It is used by members of the legal profession and describes the responsibility which one person has to another; in our particular case, that which the coach has to the student. It never ceases to surprise me how ignorant coaches are when it comes to appreciating the degree to which the law holds them responsible for what they do in a training hall. A student pays a fee to be trained effectively; he does not give his permission to be assaulted, or to be injured by poor training methods. To be sure, bruises and sprains are to be expected in any combat sport/martial art but there is a world of difference between those and injuries caused through failure in the coach's duty of care.

> Whether they realise it or not, coaches have a duty of care to young students. Training must be such as not to pose risks to them, other than those risks attendant upon any combat sport. Cases of litigation are increasing and it is a stupid coach indeed who fails to take out a coaching indemnity insurance policy!

This failure is known as 'negligence' and court actions based on it are fast becoming a serious threat to coaches. To counter this threat, many coaches are now taking out professional indemnity insurance for up to half a million pounds' cover. This is a welcome step insofar as it provides an injury victim with a likelihood of receiving some kind of financial recompense but how much better it would be if coaches were simply more aware of the dangers inherent in martial art training!

When a coach accepts a person below the age of eighteen into membership, he is taking on a duty of care – whether he is aware of it or not. He will become, in effect, that young person's guardian for the duration of the lesson and will be responsible for his well-being. His duty of care requires that he provides a safe training facility and gives suitable training. Most coaches are in default in one if not both of these areas.

Training facilities may be overcrowded, or have dangerous floor coverings. Some have hazards which intrude into the training area. The most common fault, however, is overcrowding and this has led to more injuries than just about any other training hazard. Some martial arts – such as aikido, jiu jitsu, shorinji kempo and hapkido – use matted floors because they teach throwing techniques. But throws take up much more space than punching and kicking, so a facility that will hold thirty karateka will be safe for no more than fifteen aikidoka! This fact is often overlooked.

I do not believe that matted floors are necessary for karate, tae-kwondo or kung fu practice, any more than such floors are necessary for games of five-a-side football. On the other hand, no martial arts training

> Training premises must be safe and not overcrowded. Training must be suitable to the age of the students, so it neither injures them nor equips them to injure their classmates. All equipment provided for students' use must be regularly inspected by an authorised person.

of any type should take place on a concrete or hard-tiled floor. All support pillars must be padded. Windows and glass doors should be well away from the training areas or covered with safety mesh screens. Floor areas must be kept clear of training bags.

Some coaches provide equipment for students to use. Such equipment must be regularly inspected by an authorised person to make sure it is safe. Other coaches recommend brands of equipment to students. If during its proper usage the equipment subsequently causes injury, who is at fault? Fist mitts used in karate are a good example of this! Some governing bodies have now cottoned-on and only advise students what safety features to look for when buying equipment.

To the best of my knowledge, no governing body uses a syllabus specifically designed for young people. They expect youngsters to do the same as adults and this, as you will come to see in the following chapter, is ludicrous! Young people are exercised in ways that may permanently deform them, trained in ways that could injure them for the rest of their lives and are taught dangerous techniques which they can use in the playground. The depth of ignorance surrounding the training of young people in martial art is only equalled by its extent! Fortunately, ignorance is no defence and the veil has been lifted by more socially responsible bodies such as the Martial Arts Commission.

Under the circumstances, then, what advice can I offer the would-be young martial artists and their parents? Simply this:

– no matter what the degree of competence claimed by a club instructor or association, do not join a club which is not affiliated to the Martial Arts Commission or British Judo Association;

– buy a Martial Arts Commission licence at enrolment. The licence contains a personal accident insurance and a member-to-member indemnity;

– get the address of the chief instructor of the association you join and if your club coach fails to give you satisfaction on any point of concern, then refer it to that chief instructor. If this fails, refer your complaint to the Martial Arts Commission;

– notify the coach if the young person has any health condition which might affect his participation in martial art. Particularly relevant are such conditions as diabetes or asthma.

A Suggested Code of Conduct For Training Young People

All reputable governing bodies of martial art could have no hesitation in agreeing to the following Code:

1. A young martial art club member has the right to regular training. If there is a change in venue or time, then reasonable notice must

be given. If the change is long-term and makes continued training impossible, then a portion of the annual membership fee must be refunded. If a local club closes down, then the young martial artist should be offered alternative training and if this is unsuitable, then a refund of annual fees paid must be made by the parent association;

2. all membership and participation costs must be made known to the prospective young martial artist before enrolment takes place. Details of club membership, association affiliation, licences, mat fees, uniforms and grading costs must be disclosed;

3. when young martial artists attend Summer Camps or weekend events, they have a right to expect that their whereabouts will be known to their parents and that proper and safe arrangements have been made for their arrival/dispersal;

4. the training provided must be safe for young persons insofar as its regular practice is in accord with advice given by the MediMAC of the Martial Arts Commission. Young martial artists must be matched for grade and size. When they train with older and larger persons, the latter should be capable of exercising care and control;

5. techniques must be suitable to the age-range being taught and these should not stress practical application;

fig 1. The coach must closely supervise all forms of sparring to ensure that problems are detected at an early stage. (Sylvio Dokov)

6. training should include an element of mental discipline and undesirable traits such as bullying or unreasonable aggression should be weeded out;

7. training should exclude any element of religious, philosophical, racial, sexual or political indoctrination;

8. young persons must be closely supervised at all times by the coach or his assistants. Class size should not be so large as to dilute this supervision unduly;

9. activities such as free sparring require even closer supervision and any child in distress must be immediately withdrawn (*fig 1*);

10. certain minor injuries are an inevitable consequence of vigorous martial art training. Young martial artists have a right to adequate first aid for any injury which they report to the coach.

> No reputable club or governing body would hesitate in accepting the ten point Code suggested to safeguard the rights of the young martial artist. If any do object, then the student should not enrol there.

All parents and guardians must ensure that the club which their children wish to attend agrees with this Code.

Fitness & The Young Martial Artist

The Growing Martial Artist

'Children are not miniature adults!' So says Doctor James Canney of the Martial Arts Commission. This fact is simply not understood by the vast majority of martial art coaches. Doctor Canney has pointed out one essential difference between young people and adults; that is, children are growing.

Rate of growth is not constant; for example, boys can almost double their weight in as little as two or three years (between the ages of fourteen and sixteen). With girls, this growth spurt comes two to three years earlier and explains why an average thirteen-year-old girl is bigger and stronger than a boy of the same age. Coaches should take note of this fact.

Growth is not precisely correlated with increase in muscular strength and this often leads to clumsiness and weak execution of techniques which could previously be performed well.

Physical precocity should not be confused with mental maturity and young martial artists may have a much younger outlook on life than their physical frame appears to indicate.

Children are GROWING. This affects the way they respond to fitness training. Most children are fit enough for martial art training without needing any supplementary programmes. Adult fitness programmes can actually injure the child!

Fitness

Adults usually need some form of supplementary fitness training to help them sustain skill acquisition during an intensive training session. The programme which they receive relates to their present fitness level and the effect of its application can be measured by such things as heart rate. This form of calibration cannot be applied to the growing tissues of young people.

Aerobic training allows adults to produce the number of technique repetitions necessary to 'groove in' skill. Anaerobic training provides shorter-term intensive bursts of energy as techniques are performed with maximum power. Local muscular endurance training helps over-stressed muscles to improve. Flexibility training allows limbs to move freely through their full range of movement and strength makes those movements more powerful. So much for adults!

Young martial artists need very little in the way of fitness training. Indeed they are simply not capable of some training routines! Children have all the aerobic endurance needed for an average training session and there is no need to devise additional routines. If the child cannot cope with a low-intensity session that other equivalent youngsters are finding easy, then the coach must pull that youngster out and find out what the problem is. Rigorous training does have an unfortunate habit of uncovering unsuspected weaknesses in health!

Young martial artists have no anaerobic endurance capability. If they are forced to work at high intensity, they tire very quickly and stop training. This is not laziness! Coaches must recognise this and alter routines accordingly. Endurance comes from the relative proportion of different muscle fibre types in the body. Thus red fibres support aerobic activity whilst white fibres make anaerobic work possible. This differentiation into fibre types does not occur until puberty and it appears that children have few, if any white fibres. It therefore follows that they are physiologically incapable of sustained high intensity training.

Tony Gummerson considers that most people reach their peak of power delivery in martial arts between the ages of twenty and thirty. Powerful techniques impose a great strain on young tissues and permanent damage can result if too much emphasis is placed on this aspect. Other aspects of training should therefore be stressed. As long as the technique profile is correct, then speed and strength will develop as the body matures.

Young martial artists differ most markedly from adults in their bone structures. Children's bones are still growing and contain large amounts of cartilage. Cartilage is soft, tough and resistant to breaking. It deforms rather than breaks and developing bone then takes up that deformed shape. Bone grows from plates embedded in cartilage. If these plates are damaged or displaced by bad exercises and training, then growth ceases and the limb becomes permanently stunted. If this damage occurs only to one of the two bones in the forearm or lower leg, then the other undamaged bone keeps growing and the limb becomes permanently deformed. The earlier this injury is sustained, the greater the deformity produced.

Joints between bones are of different types. Flexibility is determined by the type of joint, the tension of the muscles acting through it and the length of the ligaments which hold the joint together. Bearing in mind the points just made with regard to bone, all flexibility training for young martial artists should be approached with caution. Is it necessary anyway? Most young martial artists have no shortage of hip abduction or shoulder extension and their spines are already capable of the most amazing range of movement. Nevertheless, for reasons best known to themselves, some coaches seek to improve flexibility still further.

However, ill-advised training will not only stretch the muscles which locate the joints – making them weak and the joint unstable – it will also stretch the ligaments. Young martial artists have very elastic ligaments but these can be over-stretched. When this happens, minute tears develop and these are subsequently repaired with connective tissue. Connective tissue is not elastic and contracts as it matures, so flexibility can actually be permanently reduced.

Young martial artists respond in a characteristic way to skill training. Their nervous systems are growing along with the rest of their tissues and until the ages of eight or nine they will not have much voluntary control over actions requiring accuracy. A head kick can become a highly dangerous technique when taught to very young martial artists! This situation is aggravated during growth spurts, when a sudden extension in the limbs is not matched by a corresponding increase in co-ordination. It is why young martial artists are often clumsy.

Injuries In Training

Dr. Canney reports that a high proportion of injuries are not reported to the coach. A third of the children he examined during a survey were suffering from some form of injury which could have a permanent effect on them. Whilst there is no evidence to suggest that these injuries were caused by martial art training, the point is that the coaches were unaware of them. The coach must ask if anyone has suffered an injury – not just during martial art training but at any time. If any affirmatives show up, then the coach must decide whether they should be allowed to train or not. When in doubt, medical evaluation should be sought and the parents or guardians informed.

Such prudence on the part of the coach will do much to reduce the time taken for injuries to clear up and means that the youngster is returned to full training all the more quickly.

Motivation

Why do young people join a martial arts club? The main reason is that they have a sibling or parent who has practised/is practising. Alternatively they have seen a martial arts film and would like to be able to leap about and generally bash people they don't like, without getting bashed in return. Whatever their reason for joining, one thing is certain and that is, if they don't enjoy it, they won't stay! They stop enjoying it when they are asked to do things which they either cannot cope with, or don't want to do. The coach who wants to keep young members will first of all make their training safe, then he will make it enjoyable.

16

Statistics show that young martial artists prefer training with others in the same age bracket. High grade youngsters are an exception. These enjoy training with adults, since it often gives them a chance to help their less skilled elders. The majority of lower to middling grade youngsters, however, train longer and fare better in special classes. If a suitable syllabus is devised – as indeed it should be – then it becomes very difficult anyway to integrate them into an adult class.

The major problem faced by coaches is how to deal with the all-too-common 'Right, I've learned that, now what do we do next?' Young martial artists soak up interesting tasks like a sponge but it is the devil's own job to keep them practising these and improving their skills. The artless coach will simply force them to repeat the same old thing for session after session with the result that in a short time they have all left to take up gymnastics or badminton. It is this factor above all that militates against integrated adult/young people classes. Young people need a faster turn-over of technique. Moreover, that technique must be disguised as different games, so the students are learning skills without even being aware of it!

The keen young student will get almost totally absorbed in training, to the exclusion of all else.

Stress

Dr. Canney believes that young martial artists have no ambition of their own; this is always imported from someone else, such as a respected teacher or parent. Consequently, any child who fails has to take on board the fact that he or she has also let down a third party. In some cases, this sense of failure can prove intolerable.

Stress is a psychological tension which occurs in anticipation of having to do something, or to have something done. Stress is not necessarily a bad thing, since it prevents us from falling asleep when it is not expedient to do so. Having said that, excessive stress can pose a problem to the young martial artist. How does it arise? The simplest explanation is that a demand being made upon a young person is seen by that young person as being beyond his/her capabilities. It does not matter whether the coach considers the demand reasonable; it is how the student sees it that counts.

Some young people are naturally more anxious and stressed-up than others. These will find the prospects of gradings or competitions much more daunting than their 'laid-back' colleagues. When young students take part in a competition or grading, they know that they are being assessed and this may have an adverse effect upon their performance. This is one of the reasons why external examiners at gradings need to be properly briefed by the club coach. One particularly bad episode may be sufficient for a child to decide he has simply had enough.

The wrong kind of martial art practice creates anxiety and gets rid of young martial artists. Forcing young people into competition or sparring is a major cause of turn-over. Some children enjoy measuring themselves against others in a competition area; others do not. The good coach identifies the two categories and doesn't pressure the good performer but reluctant competitor. The coach's actions and behaviour reflect his opinion and this is soon picked up by the anxious young martial artist. Sometimes the coach doesn't have to say a word, his expression alone is enough to affect the child's perception of himself.

> Avoid stressing children by forcing them to do things which they do not want to do. Little Johnnie may be a good competitor but if he doesn't want to be, then all YOUR ambition will do is to force him out of the club.

Anxious children should be allowed to measure their abilities privately and if possible, against their own performance of a week ago. In such cases, a training record book is invaluable. Continuous assessment is less worrying than an all-or-nothing performance during a grading.

The child will do much better when he achieves pre-set goals. For example, the skilled coach will ask a young martial artist to try and kick five centimetres higher over the course of the next three weeks. In setting this goal, the coach knows it will be achieved; the youngster sees that it has been achieved and is motivated to do even better. The child is not threatened by the task set, anxiety is staved off and pleasurable anticipation sets in.

Advice on Diet

The young person is capable of putting away a great deal of food in the course of a day. This is particularly noticeable after a hard training session. Parents and guardians should therefore provide an adequate supply of protein for new tissue growth. This may be a problem for a girl, where there is a social pressure to keep weight down. If she yields to these pressures and cuts down on proteins, then the effects may become apparent in training.

For those young martial artists who dislike meat, a vegetarian diet and dairy food together can provide all the protein and vitamins required. Provided a well-balanced diet is taken, then there is no evidence to support the taking of supplementary vitamins.

Ability

How does the coach measure the rate of progress of his young students? Does he use performance at gradings, or in competitions? Whichever the method chosen, some students will prove better than others. Does the coach then concentrate on the top performers? Rest assured that the coach who does has a higher turn-over in students than the coach who encourages and motivates the clumsy and unskilled performer.

The successful coach's reputation is gained not through the number of young champions he produces but through the large numbers of young students who stay with him through the years and become valued members of the club.

Students below the age of eight may experience difficulty with adult-imposed rules and this is why they should never be involved in competition of any sort. In fact the recommended lowest age limit for participation in any form of competition is twelve. Some martial arts/medical practitioners would prefer to have that hiked up to eighteen!

Summary

Having read the previous section, you will know that children do not require the same auxiliary fitness regimes as adults. Even when there is an obvious shortcoming, it is very difficult to measure that improvement which occurs as a result of the regime. Just to recap on fitness for children below the age of twelve:

Stamina: children's muscles cannot sustain anaerobic high-intensity work. Do not work them too hard and allow frequent active rest periods, diverting them into an activity which works other muscles. Avoid speedplay and interval training;

Strength: it is not advisable to implement a formal strength training regime, though games can be used to accustom young muscles to increasing loads. Avoid press-ups and weighted squats;

Speed: children lack the neuromuscular co-ordination needed to perform techniques quickly and with sufficient skill. Discourage full-power techniques since these can damage tendon attachments and ligaments;

Suppleness: most children have sufficient suppleness for any martial art. Avoid specific flexibility routines because these can irreversibly stretch ligaments and permanently damage joints;

Agility: many children are clumsy because they lack a fully developed neuromuscular system. Agility games are helpful in this respect;

Skill: provided that a technique does not require a high standard of strength, speed and suppleness, then there is no reason why the young martial artist should not perform it skilfully;

Social Interaction: though not a physical trait, this desirable feature – where children are able to work as individuals but within a co-operative framework – can be trained in through suitable games practice.

Fitness Games I

Before any training takes place, the students should be properly dressed in loose, comfortable clothes. Teeshirts and shorts or tracksuit bottoms are excellent for this purpose. Though it is regarded as unfashionable and militaristic, I am nevertheless very much in favour of a standard low-priced training tunic. This removes the distinction which might otherwise exist between children of different income groups. Sweatshirts or club tracksuits should be worn during lulls in training.

Warm-up

This is an essential part of the adult training schedule but it fulfils a different function with young martial artists. For a start, they are likely to be more active than their adult colleagues and will have been rushing about at every opportunity. There is therefore no need to accustom their tissues to the demands of training to the same extent. Warm-up does, however, have an important psychological function because it is when the coach narrows down the students' attention to the training. What is O.K. in the playground is not O.K. in the training hall, so the warm-up is used to obtain the correct, co-operative frame of mind.

The coach must always stand in one place when he calls for a halt. When training out of doors, he should not stand so that the sun is shining into his students' faces and neither should he stand so that interesting things are happening behind him. The children should be gathered in a 'u' shape around him, with those in front sitting cross-legged. The coach always uses the same signal to stop activity – clapping the hands is a good way to be heard above the noise of children's voices. Train the students to stop immediately by playing attention games.

Send the students to the far wall and turn your back on them. They move forward stealthily until you shout 'Stop!', clapping your hands and whirling around at the same time. Any that you see still moving are sent to the sidelines. This continues until the front rank is near enough to touch you. Devise harmless and non-demeaning punishments for

fig 2. Get them to spin around in the air as they jump.

students who subsequently fail to stop what they are doing quickly enough.

Spatial Awareness Games

Children often lose track of themselves when performing complex techniques involving a series of moves. They misplace the target and sometimes forget where the floor is. Spatial awareness simply tells young martial artists where they are. Tell the students to jump high into the air. When they are all doing this together, make them twist around as they jump (*fig 2*). They use the walls as reference points as you call out a series of commands such as 'quarter turn . . . full turn . . . half turn' etc. Everyone twists in the same direction, so they all land facing the same way and mistakes are easily seen.

This game also strengthens the upper leg muscles but students tire quickly and must then be switched to a game in which they use their arms. Half way through the jumping game, get them twisting in the opposite direction. As they become more skilled, shout 'left-three quarter turn . . . right-half turn . . . right-full turn', etc. This increases the degree of co-ordination needed because not only must they now turn by the correct amount but they must also twist in the same direction.

Grappling-based martial arts should use games like the 'rollalong' (*fig 3*). One student lies on her back and grasps the ankles of her partner. She raises her knees and her partner grasps her ankles in turn. They then roll along, the person on top driving the movement with a springing forward roll. This game also teaches students to tuck their heads in and curve their backs – an essential action if they are to perform roll-outs correctly (as we shall see later). Do not perform this exercise on a hard floor and do match the students for height.

fig 3. The 'rollalong' helps tell children where they are in relation to each other and the floor.

fig 4. The kata of karate require a very precise knowledge of where each part of the body is in relation to other parts. (*Sylvio Dokov*)

Kinaesthetic Awareness Games

This is an even more imposing title but once again, it has a simple meaning. Many martial arts require the accurate adoption of formal stances and postures. Nowhere is this more evident than in the kata of karate (*fig 4*) and the poomse of taekwondo. Young martial artists have little knowledge of where exactly their arms and legs are in relation to each other. We would say that they have a low level of kinaesthetic awareness.

Kinaesthetic awareness is developed by repeatedly putting the body into exactly the right posture and holding it there, so the student comes to recognise the feel of it. An easy way of doing this with youngsters is to make one of them the teacher and the other the student. Show them a stance that you want copied (*fig 5*) and point out the mistakes to avoid. Then ask half the class to take up the stance and the other half to correct them. Correction is made by testing the stance in certain approved ways, to make sure it is stable.

Naomi has taken up a forward punching stance and this can be tested in three safe ways. The first is to press against the extended fist (*fig 6*). If the stance has the correct weight distribution and length, Naomi will be able to withstand Jennie's push. If the stance is too short, her front foot will lift (*fig 7*). Too much weight on the front leg means that a push from the rear will lift the back foot (*fig 8*) and a stance that is too wide is

fig 5. Naomi has taken up a forward stance.

fig 6. Jennie tests the stance in the first way by pressing against the extended fist. Naomi resists, keeping her shoulder low.

22

fig 7. Naomi's stance is too short, so the front foot lifts.

fig 8. Naomi's stance has too much weight over the front foot, so the rear lifts easily.

fig 9. This time Naomi has adopted too wide a stance.

unbalanced in a diagonal direction by a push against the leading shoulder (*fig 9*). Note that in all cases the correction is a simple physical one.

Give them about twenty seconds to correct their partners, then begin again. Change roles after five repetitions. The student gets five chances to feel the correct posture; the 'teacher' learns what faults to look for. As skill improves in the class, so you can set more difficult stances to correct.

Shape Games

This is a concept which I have adapted from gymnastics. Key martial art techniques involve certain body positions which must be assumed before each technique can be performed correctly. Unfortunately if the coach does not know the syllabus techniques, then he will be unable to identify these shapes and develop exercises to teach them. Thus in certain types of front kick, the back is arched but if I tell the students to 'arch their backs', what will the eight-year-old think I mean? I can go around and put everyone in the correct shape (this takes a long time), or I can refer them to a familiar game. Once they recall the game, they will self-correct.

> Use games to train in elements of martial art practice, so when you ask for a particular position to be adopted, the children know what you mean because you link it with a game they enjoy.

There are three ways to teach back arching for the relevant front kick. The first is the 'bridge' (*fig 10*, right of frame). Jennie brings her hands to the side of her head and pushes her body off the ground, taking the weight on her palms and soles. Under no circumstances should she take the weight on her head. Choose this exercise for older students and if anyone experiences difficulty, switch them to the 'ankle pull' (*fig 10*, left of frame). Naomi has folded her legs back and grabbed her feet, arching her back until her thighs and chest are clear of the mat.

fig 10. (Right of frame) The head must not rest on the floor during the 'bridge'. (Left of frame) 'Ankle pull' is a simpler way of learning how to arch the back.

fig 11. Carl 'flies' into a back hyper-extension.

fig 12. Stephen flies to the right.

Most popular is the 'Superman' exercise, first described to me by John White of Gymnastics. Carl lies on his stomach and 'flies', with fingers and toes fully extended (*fig 11*). Tell Stephen to fly to the right and he will turn his body, bringing his right arm to his side (*fig 12*); similarly for the left. Try to get a child to perform a hyper-extension (which is what this exercise actually is) and in five seconds he'll be puffing, panting and bored. Get him to play Superman and you'll have difficulty making him stop!

This exercise also strengthens the muscles of the spine but since that is not its purpose, I have placed it in this section of the warm-up.

The 'aeroplane' is a key game for developing the spinal torsion needed to perform a roundhouse kick. Begin by getting students to extend their arms to the side like aeroplane wings. Then have them run around, turning and banking away by twisting their bodies as they raise one arm and lower the other (*fig 13*). Urge them to ever tighter turns/banks, so one 'plane' turns inside the other. Sharpness of turn is signalled by the height of the outer arm.

fig 13. 'Aeroplane' shows how to shape the body for a roundhouse kick.

fig 14. David uses explosive action to thrust himself high into the air.

fig 15. Jennie folds forward and tries to touch her toes before she lands.

fig 16. Naomi performs a single leg hop, folding her left leg into a half-lotus.

Jump Games

Jump games ready the legs for hard work. It would be unwise to include explosive work early on into an adult warm-up but children are far more active and take readily to it. The object is not to tire them, so individual students should be allowed to drop out when they want. Both grappling and impact martial arts use explosive leg movements, so it is up to the coach to design the most appropriate for his purposes. These exercises can be combined with the appropriate spatial awareness training.

In the first exercise, David jumps high and tucks his knees up (*fig 14*). In the second, Jennie tries to touch her toes whilst still airborne (*fig 15*). In the third, Naomi does a single leg hop, her other foot pulled up into a semi-lotus position (*fig 16*). This also teaches balance.

The students bob down before they spring up (*fig 17*) but they should never be allowed to flex their knees more than 90 degrees, since this strains knee ligaments and muscle tendons.

Strength Games

These are nothing like the formal strength training systems of adults. They simply work the muscles which will be used during training proper. Each martial art has different requirements and the coach must decide which exercises are appropriate. In the first example, Jennie grasps Naomi's ankles and 'wheelbarrows' her up the training hall (*fig

fig 17. Limit knee flexion to 90 degrees to avoid overloading the joint.

27

fig 18. 'Wheelbarrows' are a fun way of working the shoulders.

18). The method shown is to be used for experienced students only. For new students, the legs are grasped at the knees so if the 'wheelbarrow' collapses, the supporter prevents the child from falling onto his face (*fig 19*). The wheelbarrow proceeds at the pace of the supported, rather than the supporter. Wheelbarrow races must take place on mats!

'Reverse wheelbarrow' varies this theme. Carl lifts Darren by his shoulders and the latter scuttles along as quickly as he can go (*fig 20*). This produces gales of laughter whilst working the muscles used in reverse sweeps and hooks.

The 'donkey' is an excellent isometric neck exercise. David has interlaced his fingers behind Jennie's neck and is trying to pull her forward, Jennie digs her heels in and pulls back (*fig 21*). The 'tugalong' game is similar but it does not use the neck muscles. David and Steven

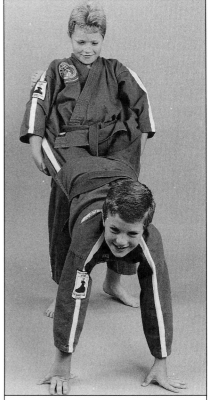

fig 19. Be prepared for the 'wheelbarrow' to collapse by holding onto the thighs.

fig 20. 'Reverse wheelbarrow' works muscles on the backs of the legs.

fig 21. The 'donkey' strengthens muscles on the back of the neck.

have interlaced fingers and are each trying to tug the other forward (*fig 22*). Both rear back and dig their feet in – and both are enjoying it! 'One-arm tugalongs' do the same thing and stretch the shoulder joints at the same time (*fig 23*). 'Elbow tugalongs' work the biceps and teach how to use the forearm during blocks (*fig 24*). 'Bend-over tugalongs' (*fig 25*) work the spine but watch out – Carl is cheating by bracing against his knee!

fig 22. The 'tugalong' stretches the shoulder joints and teaches how to work against the opponent.

fig 23. 'One-arm tugalongs' strengthen a different set of muscles.

fig 24. 'Elbow tugalongs' work the biceps.

fig 25. 'Bend-over tugalongs' stretch the hamstrings but watch out – Carl is cheating!

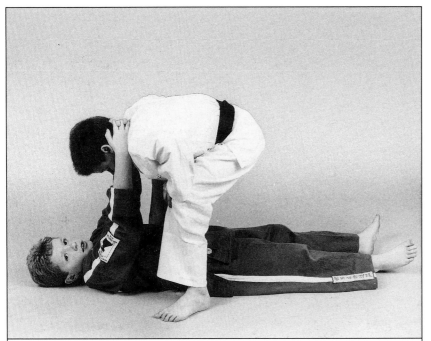

fig 26. 'Lifting the log' exercises both lifter and 'log'.

fig 27. The lifter takes the weight on his neck and back muscles. The 'log' locks his body straight.

'Lifting the log' is a multi-function exercise, working both the 'log' and the lifter. The log, in this case David, lies on his back, interlacing his fingers behind Darren's neck. Darren leans forward to facilitate this (*fig 26*). Darren straightens his knees, tenses his neck muscles and lifts David. David has to tighten his tummy muscles to prevent his bottom from sagging (*fig 27*). Perform five lifts, then change over.

'Body lifts' are also a great deal of fun as they teach how to raise the opponent prior to performing a throw. Steven has leant forward and Darren has reached down and grabbed him firmly around the middle. Darren then arches his back and thrusts his hips forward, lifting Steven high into the air (*fig 28*). Pushing actions form a major part of many throwing actions, especially when combined with knee straightening actions. Here Jennie has thrust Darren high into the air with an explosive push (*fig 29*). If she is feeling extra strong and the floor is well padded, she can throw Darren into the air. Compare this fun game with dreary old press-ups!

Suppleness Games

These involve moving the shoulder and hip joints through their full range of movement. The first is called the 'canoe'. Two students sit facing each other with their legs outstretched and the soles of their feet in contact. They each lean forward and extend their arms, hooking their fingers together (*fig 30*). More supple pairs can grasp each other's wrists. They take it in turns to lean back, drawing the other forward and

fig 28. Darren body-lifts Steven by arching his back and driving his hips forward.

fig 29. Jennie thrusts Darren high into the air with an explosive thrust of her upper arms.

fig 30. The 'canoe' requires good hamstring flexibility in that the backs of the legs are pressed to the floor.

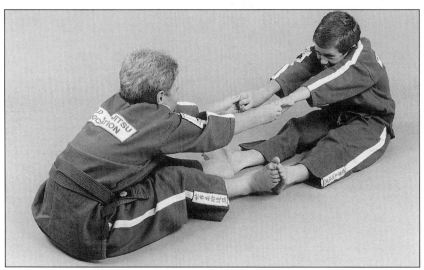

fig 31. They take it in turns to lean back, drawing the other forward. Don't let those knees bend!

fig 32. Both partners try to lift their backsides from the floor in a 'vee-sit'.

stretching the muscles on the backs of his legs (*fig 31*). Both partners must keep the backs of their legs pressed to the floor. Vary the exercise by getting both partners to pull together, so their backsides lift off the floor in a 'vee-sit' (*fig 32*).

Next open the legs but allow the soles to remain pressed together (*fig 33*). The partners work their way towards each other by successively grasping elbows and then necks. As they do this, their legs are opening wider. This exercise, which I call the 'box', requires a precise matching of leg lengths. If one partner is shorter, allow him to put the soles of his feet against the inside of his partner's ankles (*fig 34*).

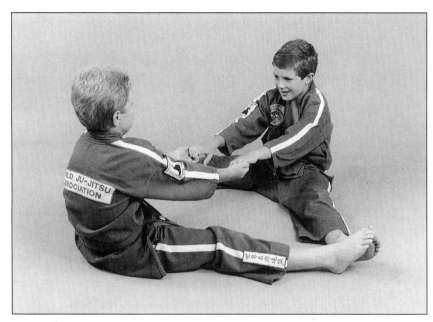

fig 33. Pull strongly in towards each other by first grasping elbows and then shoulders.

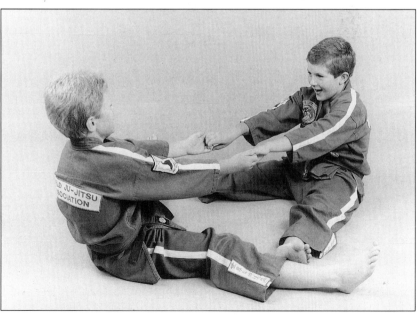

fig 34. The shorter partner can put his feet against his partner's ankles.

fig 35. Keep the elbows tightly locked together during 'crawl-over'.

fig 36. Repeat the exercise but this time with the legs open wide.

The 'crawl-over' describes an exercise where the partners sit back to back, elbows interlocked. One partner 'walks' up and over the other's back, forcing the latter's head between his knees (*fig 35*). The object is for the partner on top to touch the crown of his head to the mat. Vary the exercise by getting the partner on the bottom to open his legs wide (*fig 36*).

This brief selection of exercises represents only a fraction of those which can be devised by the good coach. They are effective and they are fun! Measure the success of the warm-up by the smiles it produces.

Warm-down

Warm-down occupies the last five to ten minutes of training. The youngsters have been working aerobically for the whole session, so their tissues will not be clogged by anaerobic waste products. The slowing tempo of physical work is paralleled by a lowering of exuberance as you prepare them to return to their everyday environments. What is O.K. in the training hall is emphatically NOT O.K. in the playground or street.

> Don't hype children up through enthusiastic training and then turn them loose on the streets! Follow all training sessions with a warm-down that returns them to a normal level of activity.

Relaxation games are quite useful though they do not hold attention as well as physical work. Stand the students up straight and tell them to imagine that there is a hook attached to the top of their heads. Tied to this hook is a large lighter-than-air balloon. They can either stand still, or walk with long, slow paces around the training hall as the balloon draws them up and makes them taller. Then tell them to stretch out on their backs, opening their arms and legs (*fig 37*). Tell them to imagine they are becoming heavier and sinking into the mat.

Whichever games you choose, aim to slow physical activity down before you let them off the mat!

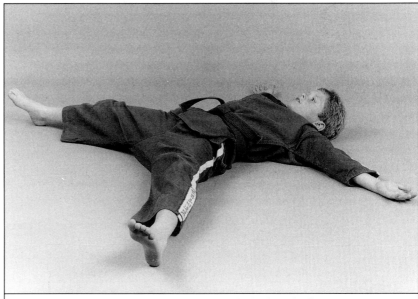

fig 37. Try to get them to imagine that they are sinking into the floor.

Fitness Games II

fig 39. Steve runs around Naomi in a tight circle as quickly as he can.

The previous chapter considered fitness games suitable for warm-up and warm-down. In this chapter we will look at a further selection of exercises to be introduced as a means of breaking up blocs of training. These are more group or equipment oriented and one of their objects is to improve social interaction. None of the martial arts is truly a team game insofar as each person relies upon another – as they do in a football match. They may use teams but the individual is all-important. Don't allow team captains to pick their own teams because they will not select weaker or less gifted students, reinforcing the latter's feelings of inferiority.

fig 38. Jennie runs quickly around her supporting arm; first one way, then the other.

Agility Games

These are intended to improve co-ordination of mind and body. They are particularly useful during growth spurts. Jennie is supporting herself on her left arm and running around it, first one way, then the other (*fig 38*). Steven runs around Naomi as quickly as he can (*fig 39*). Slalom runs around classmates are good fun, and leapfrog (*fig 40*) is a perennial favourite. More energetic youngsters should be encouraged to vault high over their partner's back, opening their legs as wide as possible. 'Leapfrog and tunnel' is a variation on this exercise. Darren is about to leapfrog over Steven's back. Naomi has just done this and is now worming her way between David's legs (*fig 41*). This exercise is performed in the form of a race between two parallel chains of players.

Put two belts down about one metre or so apart and have the students jump in a zig-zag along their lengths (*fig 42*). Repeat the exercise but this time jump from side to side. Relay jumps mean that each student jumps after an opposing team member lands on their side (*fig 43*). Begin with forward jump relays, then go to side jumps and finally to jumps and spin-arounds in the air.

fig 40. Leapfrog is a perennial favourite of young martial artists.

fig 41. Students vault over each other's backs and then tunnel between the legs of the next in line. This is performed at speed.

fig 42. Jump in a zig-zag between two spaced belts.

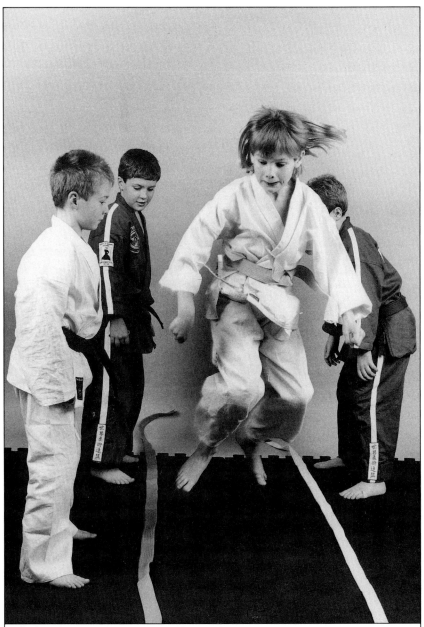

fig 43. Naomi spins around as she plays relay jumps.

Steven and Carl have stretched a belt between them and Naomi clears it with a sideways jump (fig 44). Both her legs are tucked up, as they would be if she was practising a flying side-kick. Things get a little harder for David. He has to dive between two belts, touching neither as he does so (fig 45). Naomi and her partner move their arms smoothly from 'five minutes to five' to 'twenty-five past eleven'. David will only be able to clear the belts in either of these two positions, so timing is combined with agility. Make sure the students hold the belts lightly, releasing them the instant a foul-up occurs.

fig 44. Naomi lifts her legs quite high as she easily clears the belt.

fig 45. David dives between two belts, taking care to touch neither.

fig 46. 'Sweep jumps' require timing to clear the pole as it swings.

'Sweep jumps' make use of a light plastic pipe or pole (cold water piping is ideal) to improve agility and timing. Jennie swings the pole smoothly and not too fast at her group's ankles. Each partner jumps in turn as the pole sweeps under them (*fig 46*). If anyone gets caught out, then he becomes 'it' and takes over the pole. Watch for over-enthusiastic pole-users! Well co-ordinated groups are made to jump higher as the pole changes direction more quickly.

Strength Games
Remember the 'lifting the log' exercise we covered during the warm-up? This next version uses two lifters. David has taken Jennie's head, Darren her feet. Jennie must keep her whole body rigid as they lift her (*fig 47*). Get the smaller students to lift the heavier boys and girls but make sure they set the 'logs' down without too much of a bump! 'Fall guy' trains for explosive pushes by thrusting a dead weight – in this case Darren – between two 'pushers'. Notice how Steven has quite naturally brought his centre of gravity forward – as he would do if leading in to certain types of throw (*fig 48*). Carl has received the weight, springing Darren with his bent elbows subsequent to thrusting him away. Give each partner a turn as fall guy.

fig 47. Jennie keeps her body rigid as she is lifted. The lifters must set her down carefully.

fig 48. 'Fall guy' uses explosive strength to propel Darren from one side to the other.

The 'scrum' pits two teams against each other, the object being to push into the other's ground. This really is good fun and teaches the youngsters to lower their centres of gravity and dig in powerfully (*fig 49*). It is particularly useful for grappling arts such as judo and jiu jitsu.

fig 49. The 'scrum' teaches how to lower the centre of gravity when digging in.

fig 50. Tug of war is a great favourite. Here it is used to increase forearm strength and grip.

'Tug of war' is an old favourite (*fig 50*). Carl and David have interlocked their fingers while Steven and Darren try to drag them apart. This strengthens the muscles of the forearms and helps produce a firm grip. The loser is the one who releases.

Vary this exercise using a belt as the rope (*fig 51*). This builds strength and develops a healthy competitive attitude. Two belts can be tied tightly together to produce a circular tug of war (*fig 52*).

fig 51. Play orthodox tug of war using a spare belt.

fig 52. Circular tug of war doesn't take up too much room.

fig 53. 'Twister' works the muscles of the upper body in a similar way to that used in certain throws.

fig 54. Mounted wrestling needs a padded floor.

The plastic pipe re-emerges for 'twister', a game that taxes upper body strength and helps teach how to control the opponent. Both have one hand on the inside and one on the outside of the pipe. Each tries to turn the pipe through 90 degrees as the other resists (*fig 53*). Stronger performers bend their knees to sink the centre of gravity and bring their elbows in. This is exactly what is needed to take control of the opponent during formal practice.

Mounted wrestling is great fun, though you need a padded floor. The horses charge and try to hook each other's legs. The riders grapple and try to pull each other off (*fig 54*).

Light medicine balls are excellent for developing upper body explosive power. Younger students can use plastic footballs, or foam balls. Darren is leaning forward, holding the medicine ball in both hands; Steven makes ready to receive (*fig 55*). Darren straightens up suddenly and hurls the ball to Steven (*fig 56*). Steven receives the ball, drops down and throws it back.

fig 55. Darren makes ready to throw the medicine ball.

fig 56. Darren hurls the ball with an explosive movement of his back and shoulder muscles.

fig 57. A double handed thrust helps to generate the 'shrugging' action needed to make short punches effective.

David holds the ball against his chest with both hands. He makes a double handed thrust, throwing it straight to Steven (*fig 57*). This is a good exercise for impact-based martial arts of all kinds. Vary the degree of elbow flexion and try with them nearly straight (*fig 58*), throwing the ball with a shrugging action of the shoulders. This shows how to develop explosive power over shorter and shorter distances.

Reverse punch is a key technique in many martial arts and its movements can be trained in with the aid of a small ball. Steven stands in left forward stance, holding the ball in his right hand. He pulls the ball back to his right hip (*fig 59*) and then twists forward in the sequence hips/shoulders. Tell him to pull back his left hand as fast as possible and thrust out the ball (*fig 60*). Measure the distance the ball travels and give him four more goes to beat that first attempt. Repeat the exercise on the left side and if this is much weaker, give extra repetitions. The action of throwing closely parallels that of reverse punch – providing that the throwing arm is kept close by the side of the body (*fig 61*).

48

fig 58. The straighter the elbows, the more difficult it is to generate explosive strength.

Many advanced martial art techniques which would normally take months to learn can be quickly trained in using imaginative games. For example, throwing a ball quickly teaches the quite complicated co-ordination needed to perform reverse punch.

fig 59. Steven pulls the ball back to his right hip.

fig 60. Then he unwinds and thrusts out the ball with as much force as possible.

fig 61. The throwing elbow must remain close to the side of the body.

Stand everyone in a line and reach back with the medicine ball, passing it to the person behind (*fig 62*). The further the students stand apart, the more they must stretch. The ball passes from hand to hand (*fig 63*) until it reaches the end of the line, when it is passed forward between the legs of the person in front (*fig 64*).

fig 62. Each person reaches back and passes the ball to the one behind.

fig 63. The further apart everyone is, the further they must stretch when passing the ball.

fig 64. Collect the ball from between your legs and pass it forward.

fig 65. Naomi takes the ball from one side, twists around and returns it on the other.

Flexibility Games

Naomi has received the ball from Jennie by twisting around to look over her right shoulder. Now she has twisted around to her left and is returning the ball (*fig 65*). Carl and David are passing the ball to each other as quickly as possible (*fig 66*). Both of these exercises teach how to locate an opponent who is standing behind, in preparation for a seize and throw. Darren and Naomi are passing the ball to each other (*fig 67*). When each takes possession, they fold their knees and withdraw the ball, returning it promptly for the other to take.

fig 66. Carl and David pass the ball quickly to each other, twisting from side to side.

fig 67. Collect the ball, fold your knees, then straighten your legs again and pass the ball to your partner.

Bridging Games

Bridging games take the students one step closer to martial art practice proper, whilst retaining the games image. In the first sequence, Darren has settled himself into an all-fours kneeling position. David is lying across his back and tries to loop underneath him without any part touching the floor (fig 68). This makes for a powerful grip and teaches the co-ordination needed to struggle for an advantaged position.

Groundwork is an essential part of certain martial art practice and youngsters often find it the easiest of all. They are used to scuffling

fig 68. David must loop right around Darren's body without any part of him touching the floor.

fig 69. Darren 'bridges', throwing David forward and off-balance.

around on the floor and take readily to games such as the following. David has taken up a kneeling position on Darren's shoulders, with the intention of pinning him down. On the coach's command, Darren has a short time in which to dislodge David before they change over. Darren has responded by thrusting his hips up and arching his back (remember the 'bridge' exercise?), so David is thrown forward (*fig 69*). The coach must specify the particular hold-down, otherwise things sometimes get a little out of hand!

Darren and Carl are sitting back to back, waiting for the coach's command (*fig 70*). Both spin around together, the one who gets there first has the best choice of grip (*fig 71*)! They grapple on their knees, trying to make any part of the opponent touch the mat (*fig 72*).

fig 70. Darren and Carl sit, awaiting the coach's command.

fig 71. The first to spin around gets the best grip!

fig 72. The loser is the one who touches the floor with any part of his body apart from his knees and lower legs.

fig 73. David and Steven wrestle from a standing position. The first to touch the floor with part of his body other than his feet loses.

David and Steven lock arms as they begin grappling from a standing position (*fig 73*). The object, again, is to wrestle the other until any part of him other than his feet touches the mat. Naomi has been a little slow off the mark (*fig 74*) and Steven has gained the advantage. Just you wait 'til the next go!

This concludes the exercise/game sections of the book but before closing, I would like to suggest that if medicine balls and plastic pipes are hard to come by in sufficient quantities for a large class, a training circuit can be set up so each group has a go at an exercise before moving on to the next.

fig 74. Naomi fails to dig in and gets thrust back off balance.

Basic Skills I

I take the view that, with the possible exception of kendo, all martial arts should begin formal training by teaching young martial artists how to fall safely. This should be carried out on mats and if an insufficient matted area is available, then the class should be split and the group training on the unmatted floor given something safe to get on with. Grappling-based martial arts must devote a lot of time to practising safe falling and the logical place for this is during the warm-up.

There are various ways to fall safely and all begin from a prone or crouching position. This is a safe position from which to begin practice and the skills learnt can then be applied to more advanced situations. The principle of technique progression is one of the keys to training young students successfully. Not only is progression important from a physical point of view, it has psychological importance too. The child who can perform a technique perfectly under condition 'A' but fails under 'B', always has 'A' to fall back on (excuse the pun!), so his failure is never absolute. Compare this with the bad coach who uses no progression and wants situation 'B' coped with from the outset. The child who fails now fails utterly and has nothing to fall back on.

fig 75. Carl brings his right leg forward, ready to spring.

fig 76. See how he tucks his chin into his chest!

fig 77. Collect the feet quickly and leap up.

With this in mind, let's see how a forward roll-out can be taught. Carl leans forward onto his hands and brings his right leg up, ready to spring (*fig 75*). He then lunges forward, tucking his head into his chest and curving his body into an arc (*fig 76*). He tucks his feet in and rolls up onto them (*fig 77*), ready to leap up in one smooth movement. Rolling head over heels down an incline helps teach how to stand quickly, for landing safely is only half the battle. The other half lies in regaining your feet as quickly as possible.

Technique progression means that every martial art technique begins in a simple form which everyone can do; then it builds from that point. If a student fails at a certain level, he can always drop back a notch and perform the same technique perfectly again. Using this system, failure is never complete.

After a few repetitions of this, Carl is ready to show what he can really do! Steven curls up on the floor and Carl dives clear over the top of him, reaching down with his hands as he begins tucking (*fig 78*). Youngsters thoroughly enjoy this rough and tumble and as they become more adept, the height they jump over can be steadily increased. Having said that, the coach should never force an unwilling or fearful child.

Rear roll-out is also performed from a crouching position. The back is curved and the head tucked in, so the student rolls up his back and onto his shoulders. Really fast rear roll-outs roll the student right over, so he can regain his feet in one smooth movement. Rear breakfall is similar

fig 78. As confidence builds, so the height of the roll-out increases.

59

except that the rolling motion is brought to a stop. Carl crouches down and extends his arms. His head is tucked in already (*fig 79*). Then he rolls onto his backside (*fig 80*) and arrests further movement by slapping down with both palms (*fig 81*).

Carl topples his body sideways to perform side breakfall (*fig 82*). He strikes down hard with an outstretched arm as he is about to land (*fig 83*). With a little confidence the next stage can be tackled. Here Carl has grasped a prone Darren's arm and leg and pulls him onto his back (*fig 84*). Darren breakfalls with his right arm. Next Steven has dropped to all

fig 79. Carl crouches ready to roll back.

fig 80. He sits back onto his backside and raises both arms in preparation to breakfall.

fig 81. Then he slaps down hard with both arms and harmlessly dissipates the energy of landing.

fig 82. Carl raises his left arm in preparation for a side breakfall.

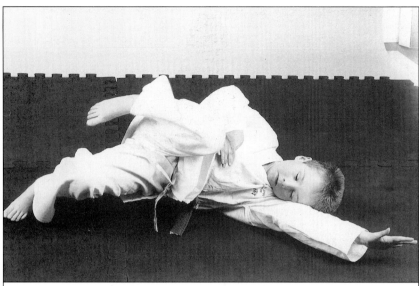
fig 83. He overbalances sideways and slaps down with his nearest arm.

fig 84. Carl drags Darren's arm, pulling him over and onto his back.

fig 85. One stage further along, Steven is kneeling on all fours when he is turned over and dumped on his back.

fours and David has taken his nearer arm and leg. He lifts them strongly (*fig 85*), dumping Steven onto his back. Steven slaps down with his right arm to cushion the landing. The following exercise will suit the real experts in the class! Carl is on all fours and Darren has taken his opposite wrist (*fig 86*). With a sudden heave, he spins Carl onto his back (*fig 87*). Carl slaps down hard with his right arm to cushion the landing.

Once students show skill at landing safely, you can introduce the game of 'push-overs'. Each student in a group takes it in turns to push everyone else over (*fig 88*). They offer no resistance and fall in whichever direction they are pushed. This game must begin softly and build in vigour as abilities rise to match. Close supervision is essential to ensure people stay away from areas of hazard such as the edge of the mat.

Body evasion games teach the key concepts of distance, timing and agility. The martial artist who controls distance is unable to be caught, yet always remains close enough to counter attack. Timing means always moving at the correct point. Too early a move alerts the opponent; too late means you get hit! The best time to move is just as the opponent begins an attack, or just after it concludes and before he has regained composure.

Split the class into matched pairs. One is 'it', attacking by advancing smoothly with an outstretched arm and attempting to touch the partner's chest. A slight pause follows each advance. The opponent can evade by moving in any one of five directions:

fig 86. Darren grasps hold of Carl's left wrist and . . .

fig 87. . . . spins him hard onto his back.

- by stepping forward into the opponent's advance and preventing it from developing;

- by stepping back from the opponent's advance, so the latter falls short;

- by stepping diagonally forward with the leading leg, drawing the rear foot up afterwards. This closes distance but takes you out of the opponent's line. Twist your body as you step and remain close to the opponent;

- by stepping diagonally back with the rear leg and withdrawing the forward foot afterwards. This increases distance and takes you out of line. Twist your body away from the opponent;

- by stepping to either side and withdrawing the trailing leg. Try to step the smallest distance commensurate with safety and turn your body. Use a block as safeguard.

Advances are first made quite slowly and only once one hundred per cent of them are being successfully evaded should the tempo increase. The evading partner may lightly touch the attacker to show that he has remained within range.

fig 88. 'Push-overs' are a practical way for training at safe falling.

One of the most important elements of any martial art is to master distance and timing. Play body evasion games to train these concepts. Students must learn how and when to move by the smallest amount commensurate with safety.

Basic Skills II

I next want to look at the subject of blocking techniques and how these can be taught in the form of games. The prime objective of a block is to prevent an attacking technique from succeeding, be that technique a grab, kick, or punch. The second objective is to block efficiently. This means expending the minimum of force to achieve the necessary deflection and in so doing, setting yourself up to make a suitable counter attack. The third objective is to perform a block which closely follows the school's stylistic notion of how a good block should be made. The third objective, I would suggest, is the least important of the three as far as young martial artists are concerned.

The usual way to teach blocks is to use the adult method. Young martial artists are put into formal stances and made to perform movements which they cannot immediately relate to. Let's see how they come across. First of all Darren is put into a straddle stance and told to extend his left arm in front of and above his head (*fig 89*). He is told to turn his blocking arm so the muscular part is uppermost whilst his

fig 89. Darren takes up a left head block, turning the soft part of his forearm upwards.

fig 90. This is the intermediate crossed arms position, where the left arm is withdrawing at exactly the same speed that the right punches upwards.

fig 91. The block is completed with a brief muscle spasm that tightens the body and makes it resistant to impact.

fig 92. Naomi instinctively blocks with a diagonal forearm held well away from the body.

right fist is drawn back to the hip. The coach next tells him to move his left arm downwards and across his face. At the same time, he thrusts his right fist diagonally upwards, so the two cross in front of his face (*fig 90*). Both arms move at exactly the same speed, so his right arm rises to blocking position as his left fist pulls to the hip (*fig 91*).

Children quickly become bored when forced to get the minutiae of style just so. Make sure they can block effectively and then bother about whether their arm should be this way or that. Games should show why certain actions are used and not others.

Compare this with the blocking game played by Naomi and Jennie. Jennie pushes a lightweight plastic tube towards Naomi's face. Almost instinctively Naomi raises her forearm and deflects it upwards (*fig 92*). She understands what she is doing and why she is doing it. Without being told, she blocks well forward of her body and achieves a good deflection. Interactive training like this teaches the meaning of distance and timing, neither of which figure in formal training. If Steven brings the tube down onto the top of David's head, he will quickly learn the value of angling his arm, so the tube slides down it (*fig 93*) rather than meeting it full on (*fig 94*). After a few goes, David instinctively rotates

66

fig 93. An angled forearm allows the blow to slide off.

fig 94. If the forearm isn't angled, it meets the full force of the descending blow.

fig 95. An x-block dissipates force by allowing the forearms to slide over one another.

fig 96. A low x-block must be performed well out from the body to stop the attack short.

fig 97. Here Carl blocks well away from his own body.

his forearm the correct way, so the delicate bones are protected. Within a short space of time, the novice learns how to x-block attacks to the face (*fig 95*) and to the stomach (*fig 96*). If you don't have enough plastic tubes to go around, then use punches and kicks (*figs 97 & 98*) instead.

I need hardly say that supervision must be such as to ensure that the plastic tube is used with restraint. For extra safety, pad the end so it is too large to poke into the orbit. But do not use so much padding that the tube becomes heavy!

fig 98. Carl leans into the block and allows his forearms to slide. His hands are pulled into tight fists and rotate so the wrists can't sprain.

fig 99. Darren makes ready to perform left lower parry.

fig 100. Blocking action is powered by pull-back of the right arm.

fig 101. Naomi turns her hips slightly away from the direction of the lower parry.

Let's now look at lower parry. The adult method puts Darren in straddle stance once more, his right arm extended and the left little finger down on his right shoulder (*fig 99*). On the command, he draws back his right arm and twists his fist palm-upwards against his ribs. This action powers a downward diagonal sweep with the left arm (*fig 100*). Switching to the equivalent game, Jennie has thrust the plastic tube at Naomi's mid section. Naomi blocks with her right arm and coincidentally has rotated her hips slightly away from the block in a way that adds power to the movement (*fig 101*). Carl turns his shoulders in the opposite direction to the block's path (*fig 102*). This also produces a faster action that cannot be trained in using the formal method.

fig 102. Carl leans into the block and his forearm strikes the side of David's leg.

fig 103. Darren drops his right arm down and across his stomach.

Darren performs a formal outer block by dropping his right arm down and across his stomach (*fig 103*). He then pulls back his left fist and brings his right forearm up in a windscreen wiper-like action that bats an attack to the outside of his body (*fig 104*). Naomi responds to an attack by performing the same action (*fig 105*) except that she can readily see why her elbow must be bent at 90 degrees, and why her fist should not lead her elbow. If David blocks with his elbow bent too much, the tube will be very close to his body when he blocks it (*fig 106*) and a slow response means he gets tapped on the chest. If he doesn't bend his elbow sufficiently, then his forearm fails to sweep a wide area and again he may get hit (*fig 107*). Failing to keep the wrist and elbow in line means that the tube is knocked down and strikes the stomach (*fig 108*). While these are self-evident after a few minutes of games practice, they are a mystery to Darren.

fig 105. Naomi blocks with her elbow well bent and her forearm out from her body.

fig 104. Then he swings his arm up in a blocking action that sweeps his stomach and chest clear of attacking techniques.

fig 106. David has flexed his elbow too much and has no space in which to deflect the attack.

fig 107. This time David's elbow is not flexed enough, so the block misses.

fig 108. Here David's fist has led his elbow in the blocking action and the attack is not deflected.

fig 109. Darren raises his right fist and brings it to the side of his head.

fig 110. Blocking action is powered by pull-back of his left arm.

fig 111. Naomi quickly learns how to block effectively against a lightweight plastic pipe.

Finally Darren demonstrates inner block, extending his left arm and bringing the right fist to the side of his head (*fig 109*). He draws back his left fist, using this action to power an inswinging forearm block (*fig 110*). This suffers from the same faults as the previous technique and these are quickly corrected using the tube (*fig 111)* or a punch (*fig 112*).

Kung fu blocks too can be practised in an interactive way (*fig 113*). Notice how Naomi quickly learns to incorporate body evasion with the blocking action, as a means of putting extra distance between her and the tube. This concept would otherwise be difficult to get across to a young student.

There are various other ways of practising blocks. Carl and Steven are working from a kneeling position. This means that neither can move his body out of the way, so the blocking action is all-important. Large circular movements are used to sweep as wide an area as possible. Carl

fig 112. Carl means business and turns his hips into the block, making it stronger.

fig 113. Naomi uses body evasion to twist her body as she deflects the pipe with a forearm block.

fig 114. Kneeling down prevents body evasion, so full reliance is placed upon blocking.

fig 115. A two handed grab is foiled by a double block.

fig 116. Carl puts his hands on his head between successive attacks.

fig 117. Notice how he twists his body during the deflection.

reaches forward to grab Steven's jacket, only to have his arm batted to the side (*fig 114*). Double blocks are extremely difficult to teach because they require a contra-rotation of the arms; this blocking game can make them simple (*fig 115*).

For the more advanced student, upper body evasion and power development are improved by twisting the body but not moving the feet. Carl puts his hands on his head and faces Steven (*fig 116*). Steven makes a grab for Carl's jacket. Carl twists his shoulders away and scoops down with his left arm (*fig 117*). Pausing briefly, Steven then punches with his right fist, only to have it blocked in a similar manner by Carl's right arm (*fig 118*). Use elbow blocks to train in body action. Carl puts his hands on his hips and faces Steven (*fig 119*). Steven punches but his blow is deflected when Carl twists his body (*fig 120*). Note that Carl keeps his hands on his hips the whole time.

fig 118. Now he twists in the other direction and blocks.

fig 119. Hip action forms the basis of an elbow block.

fig 120. Carl twists his upper body and bats Steven's punch to one side.

fig 121. Both partners must work at a speed they can manage.

The coach must closely supervise practice to ensure that both partners are working well together. The attacker must work at a speed which the defender is just capable of responding effectively to (*fig 121*). Some students will try to score points off their partner by attacking very quickly, or by feinting and then suddenly attacking. Such tactics must be stopped early on otherwise the less skilful partner will become dispirited. As far as possible, students must be equally matched (*fig 122*).

fig 122. As far as possible, students should be matched for size and ability. (*Sylvio Dokov*)

fig 123. Timing is essential when deflecting a moving target.

fig 124. Steven deflects a fast-moving ball with a head block.

Dynamic blocking games can be a lot of fun and they also improve reaction speed. A light ball is lobbed to Naomi and she responds with a forearm block that sends it flying (*fig 123*). Steven uses a head block to deflect it (*fig 124*). Games like this are enormous fun and test practical blocking ability in a way that formal methods cannot. As I stated earlier, the primary objective is to deflect the attack and if your students can knock a fast-moving ball out of the air, then they aren't doing badly at all!

Basic Skills III

Punches

In this chapter, I would like to look at some basic techniques taken from various martial arts, together with the technique progressions needed to achieve their proper performance. The first of these is the basic punch. I am not in favour of teaching under twelve-year-olds the principles underlying a punch which might be used in the playground. Therefore all punches should be of the basic 'straight arm' type and stress a thrusting action which employs little muscular action and positively no focus.

We will follow the system used in the previous chapter and begin by seeing how formal adult training introduces the basic punch. A traditional straddle stance is used and Darren extends his left fist whilst 'cocking' the right against his ribs. He brings his left fist into the centre, turning it palm downwards-facing, the right fist is turned palm-upwards. Darren relaxes his shoulders and stands ready (*fig 125*). On the coach's command, he withdraws his left fist and advances the right by an equal amount (*fig 126*). His arms move at equal speeds and the

fig 125. Darren advances his left fist, pulling the right back to his hip.

fig 126. The withdrawing and advancing fists pass each other at the mid-way point.

fig 127. Both fists twist simultaneously as the punch concludes.

fig 128. David and Steven link hands.

fig 129. Then they take turns quickly withdrawing their arms in a pull-me-pull-you alternating sequence.

fig 130. The belt loops around a wallbar, so the arms must travel at exactly equal speeds. Pull-back is more important than the punching action.

elbows remain close to the body. The punch completes as the right arm fully extends and the fist rotates palm-downwards. At exactly the same time, the left fist locates on the left hip and twists palm-upwards (*fig 127*).

As it stands, this is a fairly complicated series of movements and young students will find it very difficult to move their fists at the same speed. The easiest way to remedy this is to play 'trains' by putting David and Steven facing each other at an arm's distance apart. Each extends his left arm and they link hands (*fig 128*). As David pulls back his left hand, he draws Steven's right arm out (*fig 129*). Both use only pulling actions; no pushing of the extended arm is allowed.

Another way of teaching this is to pass a belt around a wallbar and then to grasp each end in a fist. David extends his left fist and pulls back the right to his hip, adjusting the length of belt held so it is under tension (*fig 130*). As soon as he pulls his left arm back, the right is drawn out at an exactly equal speed. Use this training method if an unequal number of students are practising and one is unpartnered for the 'train' game.

Adult training soon begins to develop speed and power as the necessary co-ordination appears. An explosive breathe-out together with muscle spasm locks the elbow joint and produces a 'focus' of effort. This focus should be avoided when training youngsters because it can damage the elbow joints. All arm extensions should be smooth and relaxed, stopping well before the elbow straightens fully (*fig 131*).

Though this may be anathema to traditional coaches, it is essential that speed and power are omitted from these 'unloaded' punches – not only for the students' sake but also for the sake of non-practising playmates. Power can be trained in later, once punch-profile is correct.

As I mentioned in the chapter dealing with exercises, reverse punch is best trained with a foam ball. Before long, students naturally use forward arm pull-back, hip action and a slight forward movement of the centre of gravity to achieve maximum distance throws. These are the fine points of reverse punch technique and normally take months of formal training to groove-in. Yet they can be learned within weeks by using a light ball.

Some coaches want to train-in additional facets, such as control and accuracy. When devising methods, the coach must not use such aids as impact pads because if he does, his students will learn how to hit hard! Instead, all impact training must be done against light targets such as a tennis ball suspended by string from a broom handle (*fig 132*). This requires accurate timing and ranging but it neither scuffs the knuckles, nor develops a powerful impact.

> It is possible to teach children how to punch and kick without teaching them how to punch and kick EFFECTIVELY. All impact techniques should be taught in a smooth pushing or thrusting manner. Techniques which develop a respectable shove are quite different from those which literally explode on the target.

fig 131. The elbow must never be allowed to straighten fully during an unloaded punch.

fig 132. A tennis ball improves accuracy without developing power.

fig 133. Children find high kicks relatively easy to do.

fig 134. The first action in front kick is to pull the knee up. Practise this action whilst keeping the sole of the foot parallel to the floor.

fig 135. Darren changes his guard and lifts his foot well clear of the belt held by Steven and Carl.

fig 136. Darren's knee drops as he thrusts his leg straight, striking with the sole of the foot.

Kicks

Children have quite flexible hips and high kicks are all too easily learned (fig 133). This is why kicking techniques must be muzzled. Skill is developed but power is omitted. Adult front kick is delivered with a snapping action, thrusting the ball of the foot deep into the opponent. In my view, coaches should teach young martial artists to kick with the sole of the foot delivered with a pushing action. All kicks should be taught from a basic stance.

Naomi practises for front kick by pulling her left knee up (fig 134). If her balance is bad, she can practise whilst lying on her back. Each knee is raised alternately and held for a second or two. The next phase is to move the kicking hip forward as the foot is raised. Darren changes his guard and his trailing foot easily clears the belt held by Carl and Steven (fig 135). Darren's knee rises higher than the opponent's mid-section and then drops as the lower leg thrusts out in a straight, pushing action (fig 136). Jennie practises leg extension by lying on her back and kicking into the air (fig 137). This helps her to perform the action correctly without worrying about balance.

fig 137. Jennie practises the kick extension lying on her back.

fig 138. Thrusting against a target teaches Steven how to concentrate his weight.

fig 139. David lifts his right leg to the side and pats his ankle.

The hips must be used correctly, so power is transmitted in a straight line to the target. David crosses his arms over his chest. Steven lifts his foot and places it against the centre of the crossed arms, then he applies thrust (*fig 138*). Steven must push David back without losing balance, using knee extension and hip action only.

Apart from using the sole of the foot instead of the ball, the junior front kick contains all the necessary elements for later development.

David practises for roundhouse kick by taking up a left forward stance. He lifts his right foot to the side and slaps his ankle with his right hand (*fig 139*). This teaches him to lift his foot high and to the side. When he has done this a few times, he goes on to perform an 'aeroplane' turn and bank to the left (*fig 140*). The twist in his spine encourages him to pivot on his supporting leg so his knee curves across the front in a horizontal arc (*fig 141*). Then he thrusts his lower leg out in a smooth movement (*fig 142*). He trains the height of his knee by kicking over a partner's back (*fig 143*). Practise roundhouse kick against a tennis ball on a string held at stomach height (*fig 144*) and avoid teaching head kicks!

fig 140. Then he 'aeroplanes', winding up the muscles in his sides and back.

fig 141. His knee curves across the front of his body in a horizontal arc.

fig 142. The lower leg is extended as the knee points at the target.

fig 143. David practises for knee lift by kicking over a prone partner's back.

fig 144. Kicking against a tennis ball improves accuracy.

fig 146. David takes up a right straddle stance and looks to his right.

fig 145. Darren gets the feel of roundhouse kick position, extending his leg and leaning away.

Darren trains for the final foot position by supporting himself on one arm whilst extending the kicking foot (*fig 145*). This helps him to recognise the feel of the correct position, with the body leaning away in line with the extended leg.

Side thrusting kick should be taught from a straddle stance, with a smooth pushing action. David takes up the stance and looks to the right, carrying both fists closed and ready (*fig 146*). On the command, he lifts his right knee until it is above the height of the target. He points his right heel at the imaginary opponent's stomach (*fig 147*) and thrusts his leg out straight with a smooth action (*fig 148*). His supporting foot swivels as the hips engage though he will not learn this action until he practises the kick against his partner's crossed arms (*fig 149*). A little bit of resistance soon produces the correct body-shape.

Sticking Hands

This is the name given to a form of practice used in certain schools of kung fu. In my view, it is very suitable for teaching to children of all ages because whilst appearing 'martial arty', it involves no dangerous techniques. It improves reaction time and builds co-ordination through a progressively more difficult series of techniques. At the present time there are no specific sticking hands routines for young students, so the following are offered as a foundation upon which development can take place.

fig 147. His knee is high enough so the heel points towards the target.

fig 148. The kicking action is a smooth thrusting push.

fig 149. Body position is checked by thrusting against a target.

fig 150. David and Steven press the backs of their wrists together.

fig 151. Steven yields to the thrust but steers David's hand to the side.

fig 152. First to break contact with the other's wrist is the loser.

90

The first sequence involves just one hand and the body remains stationary. David and Steven take up high stances and put the backs of their right hands together (*fig 150*). The hands are open and the fingers fully extended. David pushes forward with his right arm, straightening the elbow and trying to push Steven back. Steven yields to the thrust by bending his elbow and keeping the back of his hand pressed against David's (*fig 151*). David's hand is redirected to the side of Steven's shoulder. David withdraws his hand and Steven follows, continuing on to thrust towards David's chest in a reversal of roles (*fig 152*). At no time does either student try to resist the force of the thrust, though they may re-direct it. The object is always to keep in contact with each other's wrists. Change hands after thirty seconds or so.

The second sequence is taken from tai chi chuan and uses both arms. Once again the two stand facing each other, this time with their right forearms in contact, the left hands giving support to their right wrists. Steven leans forward and pushes towards David's face. David leans back and yields to the push (*fig 153*). David takes the initiative when Steven reaches full extension and presses down on his forearm, thrusting it back and towards Steven's stomach. Steven yields to the thrust, shifting his weight over the back leg and pressing David's elbow down (*fig 154*). The roles are reversed at full extension and Steven once more thrusts at David's face.

fig 153. David leans back and guides Steven's push upwards.

fig 154. David takes the initiative and thrusts back at Steven. Steven diverts his thrust downwards.

fig 155. A sudden step will make the unsuspecting opponent stagger.

After a few practices, the attacker may suddenly step forward as he thrusts. The opponent responds by quickly stepping back an equal amount. Tactical defenders will first resist a thrust, making the attacker work hard then, as he is half-way extended, they take a sudden short back step and cause him to stagger (*fig 155*). This sequence produces some quite exuberant action and anyone yielding too slowly is likely to be pushed off balance. Watch for cheating in that the winner is not the stronger of the two but is the one who makes the other break forearm contact.

Real aces can move up to a detuned version of 'rolling hands' in which both pairs of forearms press against each other (*fig 156*). One arm is above the other and they exchange places by the lower rising as the upper falls (*fig 157*). The object is to keep the forearms in contact by applying pressure through the bent elbows. When students can do this without too much thought, allow straight thrusts with either palm into the chest (*fig 158*). Sensing the sudden change, Steven swivels his hips and turns sideways, so the strike passes along his front (*fig 159*). This is real martial art training and youngsters quickly develop the most extraordinary 'feel'. Soon they do not even bother to look at each other but sense intentions through contact alone. A potential black belt student can be blindfolded and still perform skilfully. This form of training is very rewarding for blind students.

The final stage is to step forward and back during rolling hands but don't expect students under the age of twelve to be able to manage it!

fig 156. Both forearms press against each other and the elbows are bent.

fig 157. The forearms change places in a rolling action.

fig 158. A sudden straight thrust to the chest is made.

fig 159. Steven senses the thrust and turns his hips, deflecting it across the front of his body.

fig 160. Throws should not use attacks against the joints.

fig 161. David slips his arm around Steven's back.

Throws

A great many throws are suitable for junior practice, though they must neither use pre-emptive strikes nor a final blow. They should use leverage to the body or legs only, and not attack joints (*fig 160*). Hip throws are the most common, where David slips his arm around Steven's back (*fig 161*). Then he turns away and drops below Steven's centre of gravity, making it easier to lever him over (*fig 162*). He straightens his knees and lifts slightly, so Steven is raised onto his toes and drawn diagonally over the hip (*fig 163*).

fig 162. Then he drops under Steven's centre of gravity.

fig 163. Steven is drawn diagonally forward.

fig 165. Carl is lifted up and drawn over David's back.

fig 164. David dives forward and grasps Carl's ankle. His other hand takes Carl's sleeve.

In the second example, Carl steps forward and reaches for David's lapel. David dives forward, taking Carl's sleeve in his left arm and ankle in his right. Note that David's arms are spread widely (*fig 164*). David draws Carl forward and over his back, tipping him over the other side (*fig 165*).

Leg reap is a simple but effective throw. Steven and David square up, taking hold of each other's tunic shoulders (*fig 166*). Steven suddenly pulls David forward, causing him to rear back. Feeling his resistance, Steven immediately switches to a push and steps forward to the outside of his right leg (*fig 167*). At the same time he throws his head forward, pushing with his right arm and pulling with his left. He hooks back with his right foot (*fig 168*), taking David diagonally backwards and off-balance over his supporting leg.

fig 166. Steven and David take hold of each other's tunics.

fig 167. Steven steps forward to the outside of David's foot.

fig 168. Steven throws his weight forward and hooks back with his right foot.

In the final example, David is lying at Steven's feet. He throws himself into Steven's legs and traps his ankles, so preventing him from stepping back (*fig 169*). Then he rolls against Steven's trapped legs, forcing the latter onto his back (*fig 170*).

Groundwork is tremendous fun and it is taught through a series of hold-downs/escapes. The first is a belt hold, applied when David has crawled over the top of Steven and wormed his hands under Steven's shoulders to grasp his belt. He then spreads his knees and presses down with full weight on Steven's chest (*fig 171*). Steven tries to escape by bridging and twisting his body face downwards (*fig 172*), then by backing out (*fig 173*).

Groundwork comes naturally to children and they quickly learn and use simple hold-downs and escapes. Weight is an important factor in groundwork practice so match partners carefully.

fig 169. David throws himself forward and traps Steven's ankles.

fig 170. Then he rolls against Steven's legs and overbalances him.

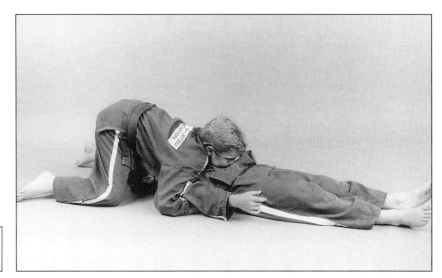

fig 171. David presses down on Steven's chest, holding him firmly by his belt.

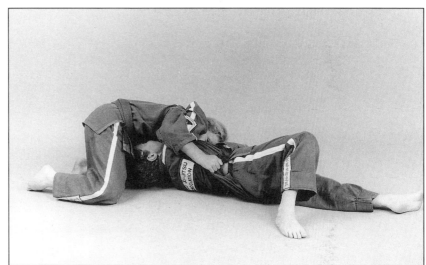

fig 172. Steven responds by bridging, then by twisting his face downwards . . .

fig 173. . . . and backing out.

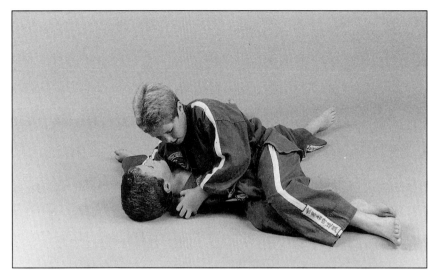

fig 174. David grips Steven's tunic shoulders and locks his arm.

fig 175. Steven responds by pushing against David's elbow and twisting violently.

The next hold-down is a cross-body hold. David has worked his way across Steven's chest and forced his right arm under his neck. David's left arm thrusts under Steven's right shoulderblade, gripping his tunic with both hands. His legs then trap Steven's right arm (fig 174). Steven escapes by wriggling and twisting violently whilst pushing against David's right elbow with his left arm (Fig 175).

Getting Started

The Martial Arts Commission

Choosing the right club is the most important step any young martial artist can take. Since there are no laws governing the practice of martial art, then anyone who wants to can simply buy a black belt and start a club. Many martial art clubs are run by people with virtually no knowledge of those arts. Consequently the standard of training offered runs from mediocre to downright dangerous. There is only one organisation in Britain which has worked for the improvement of all the martial arts. The Martial Arts Commission is to the martial arts what the BSI 'Kitemark' is to quality consumer goods.

Ignore all claims of the coach's competence except the MAC Coaching Certificate. This is your own BSI Kitemark and it gives you a right of redress in the event of complaint. Check that a local club is registered with the MAC by sending a stamped, addressed return envelope to:

The Martial Arts Commission,
Broadway House,
15-16 Deptford Broadway,
London SE8 4PE.

Or telephone 081 691 3433 during working hours.

Vetting the Club

Any reputable club will allow new members to sit and watch training. If it doesn't, then forget that particular club and go elsewhere. Is the training hall clean and spacious? Is the coach clean, well turned out and courteous? Are senior female assistant coaches on hand? Does the club run separate lessons for young martial artists? Does the club operate a special syllabus for youngsters? Does the club recognise the ten-point Code given on page 11? If the answer to all these questions is 'yes', then that is the club to join. If any 'no' answers are given, then check with the MAC before proceeding.

All clubs should use a standard enrolment form, copies of which are available from the Martial Arts Commission. This form lists the health conditions described below. If after watching training, students still wish to join, then the form should be signed by the parent or guardian. Sixteen-year-olds may be touchy about bringing their parents along to sign for them so a sympathetic coach will give them an application form to take home. No young student should be enrolled until the application form has been endorsed by the parent or guardian.

> Vet the club carefully. Is it a member of the Martial Arts Commission? Does it operate a special syllabus for children? Is the child fit enough to practise a martial art? Declare all health conditions to the coach before enrolment.

An application for an MAC licence must be completed immediately the student enrols. Statistics show that most injuries occur during the first few months of training so this is when MAC insurance cover is needed. MAC insurance protection operates in two ways. The first way is a personal accident indemnity which pays a capital sum in the event of permanent injury or death. The second is a third party liability which operates should the holder injure another young student. Despite the obvious value of this policy, many coaches do not apply for students' licences until the date of grading approaches. This is a very bad practice.

Some application forms contain disclaimer notices which seek to exonerate the club or coach in the event of injury. These notices have no force in law, since no one can sign away their statutory rights. The purpose of the disclaimer is simply to let parents and guardians know that like any other sport, the practice of martial art does involve risk. By watching a pre-enrolment session, parents and guardians can evaluate the level of risk for themselves.

Vetting the Martial Art

You may be lucky enough to have a choice of martial art clubs near you. If so, then you should read the following chapter. I have made an arbitrary separation of students into those under twelve years of age, and those over. Whilst appreciating that there will be relatively mature eleven-year-olds and childish thirteen-year-olds, I still feel that a general guideline may have some value.

In my view, twelve plussers can study most martial arts where the coach is capable of tailoring the adult session to their needs. By way of contrast, under-twelves should not enrol in any impact based martial art unless it has a special syllabus which removes potentially dangerous techniques likely to be misused in the playground (fig 176). Grappling based martial arts may also pose risks to those practising them.

Until such time as a martial arts governing body produces an

fig 176. Techniques must not be immediately applicable for misuse in the playground. (*Sylvio Dokov*)

MAC-approved syllabus of disarmed and safe techniques, I would strongly recommend enrolment only in a judo club for the under-twelve age group.

> As a rule of thumb, unmodified grappling martial arts are better for children to learn than unmodified impact-based arts. Neither, however, is as good as a syllabus specially put together for the young martial artist.

Vetting the Child

Assuming that you can find a good martial art club which passes your vetting, what about the suitability of the child? Martial art training involves knocks and bumps so the child must be robust enough to enjoy a rough and tumble. Most people are familiar with the requirements of rugby and hockey and if your child is capable of playing those, then he will find martial art training no more demanding.

Physically disadvantaged children are not disbarred from practising appropriate martial arts. Blind children do very well at judo, jiu jitsu and wing chun kung fu. Spina bifida and wheelchair users can also practise wing chun since the latter emphasizes upper body movement. Children with maldevelopment of the arm(s) will do well at taekwondo, since it emphasizes footwork.

Grand mal epileptics can participate fully in martial art training if the facility has a padded floor. The sudden onset of seizure can be perturbing for onlookers, so the other children must be made aware of the situation. Petit mal sufferers should let the coach know what form their seizures take and whether there are any behavioural clues indicating that one is imminent. Diabetics enjoy training but should always take some lemonade into the training hall. The coach should encourage the sufferer to sip the lemonade in the event of collapse and generally this will provide sufficient sugar to allow recovery. The coach must be informed if any symptoms indicate the early onset of sugar starvation.

Asthma is improved by martial art training but again, medication must be taken into the training hall. It is important that sufferers learn to distinguish between the natural breathlessness arising from hard training and the onset of an attack. The onset of an asthma attack can be very distressing for sufferer and onlookers alike, so it helps if a separate changing room is available for the sufferer to recover in.

Young cardiac students may train provided they have a clean bill of health from their doctors. Heart muscle is like any other; it responds well to the right kind of exercise.

A fit heart pumps more blood per contraction, thus allowing a faster carriage of oxygen to the working tissues.

Haemophiliacs are normally disbarred from all martial art training but on medical advice, it may be possible for them to train in tai chi chuan provided that they avoid 'pushing hands'. I have known sufferers of von Willebrandt's Disease to train without incident but again, prior medical clearance is essential.

Psychologically disturbed children may find martial art practice helpful provided, of course, that their participation poses no risk to other students. The advice of a social worker should be sought before enrolling such children.

The coach must be told at the outset about all disabilities and not be left to discover them for himself! The club must always have a trained first aider within easy reach and a first aid kit should be on hand. The location of the nearest open Casualty Unit must be known.

The coach should keep a record of all accidents occurring at the club. This should name the victim and explain in simple terms what happened. The report must also record the date and time of the accident, the number of people practising on that night, and the first aid administered. All first aid should be of a type approved by the MediMAC and no other pills or potions should be dispensed.

All emergency exits from the training premises must be clear for use. Clubs must hold regular fire drills and all evacuated children accounted for by means of a nightly register.

The Syllabus

Introduction

Techniques are not taught in a haphazard manner; they follow a carefully ordered programme which begins with basic techniques and concludes by combining basic techniques in complex ways. Basic techniques are themselves graded according to complexity into a syllabus. Each martial tradition has its own syllabus based upon particular aims and objectives. The object of the syllabus is to facilitate the structured teaching of the contents of a martial tradition to new students. For example, the syllabus of most karate schools is arranged so it teaches virtually all the fundamentals in a three year period, assuming twice-weekly training plus occasional specialist weekend courses.

Once the fundamentals have been learned, the student becomes a black belt. Sometimes the black belt is referred to as a 'martial artist'. This curious reference begs the question, can a nine-year-old become a martial artist by following the syllabus (*fig 177*)?

Too many coaches nowadays wrongly assume that the measure of a martial artist is the skill with which techniques are performed. A moment's thought, however, reveals that the skill aspect can only be a small part of being a martial artist; for what is the value of producing a skilful warrior who runs away during the battle? No, the aim of martial art training is to produce a skilled performer with a martial art mind. The martial art mind is characterised by an inclination towards direct action; that is, action unmodified by emotions such as malice, fear, or anger. These emotions adversely influence skilled performance of technique upon which personal survival depends. In practice, the adult finds it much easier to acquire skill in technique performance than to make the vital transition between mere technician and martial artist. And if an adult finds it difficult, can we expect the child to fare any better?

The answer must be a categoric 'no'; so our nine-year-old black belt mentioned above is not a martial artist. At best he is a nine-year-old child who has been trained to use potentially dangerous techniques.

fig 177. Is a nine-year-old black belt a martial artist? (*Sylvio Dokov*)

The only protection enjoyed by that child's young colleagues is the coach's strict admonishment that 'he must never use martial art technique outside the training hall!' I personally don't think that admonishment is worth very much. Accordingly I take the view that it is high time governing bodies faced up to their responsibilities to society. If they are to take in and train children, then training must be based upon a syllabus which takes into account young students' physical and mental immaturity.

The following is an analysis of the different martial arts practised in Britain by adults and it suggests how training might be amended to suit the under-twelves.

Aikido

Aikido is a grappling-based responsive martial art which attempts to divert the attacker's force in order to use it against him. It is suitable for young people insofar as the classical form does not teach how to initiate attack. It gives grounds for concern, however, because it uses attacks to the joints; specifically to the wrists. Bearing in mind the fact that the young person's wrist is a very delicate cartilaginous structure, one wonders how it might take to three hours a week of intensive twisting and pulling.

The principles of yielding to attack could be taught as the basis for a number of entertaining games and perhaps attacks on the wrist might be diluted by work against the elbow and shoulder.

Sports aikido schools might consider omitting knife defence for though only a rubber dagger is used, one cannot but help wonder whether this is nevertheless familiarising the young child with the use of weapons. Two-against-one sparring should be taught only to the twelve-plussers.

Full Contact

Full contact is the name given to a collection of striking-based martial arts which have come together for the purposes of competition. Think of them as boxing plus kicks, so if you have reservations about young people boxing, then you will definitely not approve of full contact. Gloves and padded boots are worn and though these may reduce laceration, they do little to mitigate brain damage!

Even if young students do not compete, the techniques used are all intensely practical and can be used with equal efficiency in the school playground. In my opinion, full contact is unsuitable for teaching to persons below the age of sixteen.

Hapkido

This is a Korean analogue of aikido, so the above comments are also relevant here. Hapkido also includes striking techniques, so refer to the karate section.

Jiu Jitsu

Jiu jitsu is the umbrella name for a group of styles of grappling-based martial art. One of its most famous styles is the Olympic sport of judo (see next). But whereas judo has refined its syllabus to make it suitable for young people, many jiu jitsu styles have not. A national children's syllabus must be devised and this should exclude such things as throws which use leverage against joints and striking techniques to the groin and eyes.

Judo

In my view, judo is the best martial art for the under-twelves. Though judoka will not be happy with my description, I nevertheless regard judo

fig 178. Karate kata is very ritualistic and of little immediate practical value. (*Sylvio Dokov*)

as no more than skilful wrestling. A lot of good work on children's participation has already been done and all of the dangerous techniques are now gone from the syllabus. What remains is a vigorous but largely harmless pastime that has many of the advantages of martial art practice with none of the disadvantages.

Karate

Karate is a striking-based martial art which teaches how to use the hands and feet as weapons. Though it has detuned its own techniques over the last fifty years or so, it still teaches a great number of joint-damaging kicks and punches. Within months, the karate-practising youngster will be taught how to kick a young classmate in the face, or how to attack the knee with a stamping kick. There is no national children's syllabus.

fig 179. Kendo is tremendous fun and one of the safest martial arts for young persons to practise. (*Sylvio Dokov*)

The karate syllabus should be modified to remove all emphasis upon speed and strength. Techniques should be performed smoothly and with light movements. Practical techniques, such as snapping punches delivered from fighting stances, should be eliminated from the syllabus. No head, groin, or knee kicks should be taught. Free fighting should not be taught to the under-twelves. Kata is excellent training for all ages. It is very ritualistic and of limited practical value (*fig 178*).

The same comments apply to the Korean analogue of Tang soo do.

Kendo

Kendo is the art of Japanese swordfighting but don't let that alarm you! Bamboo swords are used together with full armour. Youngsters will find the ritual and early training incomprehensible, though they will enjoy the shouting and cantering about. The training is hard and young kendoka will not be able to sustain the explosive power needed. Having said that, for those parents who can afford to buy the necessary equipment, I personally think that kendo is eminently suitable for young people. It is sufficiently divorced from real life to make its practice entirely safe (*fig 179*).

Kung Fu

Though kung fu clubs are fairly numerous, little authentic kung fu is taught in Britain. The Chinese are traditionally secretive about their martial art and masters teach the core principles of their style to only a handful of their senior students. Most of these are Chinese. So if you can simply walk into a local club and enrol a youngster, then it is unlikely that they will be taught 'the real thing'. But since young martial artists should not in any case be taught 'the real thing', then this may not be too much of a problem.

However, kung fu is afflicted with more than its fair share of dubious coaches. This has come about through the secrecy which still surrounds authentic practice. There is simply no way of checking whether a coach is good or not. Some authentic styles make much use of fist and arm conditioning, both of which would prove damaging to growing tissues. Many use hard, snapping movements which are injurious to young joints.

Kung fu is divisible into 'hard' and 'soft' styles. Some of the hard styles gave rise to karate, so the relevant comments apply here too. Parents should avoid enrolling their children in clubs which teach weaponry such as the rice flail. Soft kung fu is ideal for teaching to children because the techniques are harmless to their young tissues and take many years of assiduous practice before they can be misused effectively outside the training hall. Children find the bafflegab on 'chi' totally incomprehensible but love to practise 'pushing hands'.

> Soft Chinese styles of kung fu, wu shu, kendo, shotokai karate and kendo are all suitable for young martial artists to learn.

Ninjutsu

No authentic ninjutsu has been publicly taught for at least a hundred years though that has not prevented a small number of entrepreneurs from claiming to do just that. One look at the throwing stars, garottes and daggers employed during practice should be sufficient to deter any sane parent from enrolling their child in a 'ninjutsu' club!

Nippon Kempo

This is Japanese boxing. It is similar to full contact except that face masks and chest protectors are worn. On the debit side, there are no weight categories. As with full contact, techniques are intended to have a practical use and so may be easily misapplied. However, there is no reason why the kicks and punches cannot be taught in a 'soft' manner, in which case nippon kempo becomes quite an enjoyable martial art for young people.

Shorinji Kempo

Shorinji kempo claims to be based upon the kung fu taught in the ancient Buddhist monastery of Shaolin. It involves what for practical purposes can be regarded as jiu jitsu and karate-type techniques, so the relevant paragraphs above should be re-read. Additionally, shorinji kempo involves a certain amount of Buddhist-type indoctrination to which some parents may take exception.

Taekwondo

Taekwondo is a Korean striking based martial art and many of the comments applied to karate apply here too. However, the 'official' form of taekwondo allows competition between children and although head and chest protectors are worn, relatively forceful blows and kicks are exchanged (*fig 180*). Young children are taught how to kick strongly to

fig 180. Taekwondo teaches forceful kicks to the head. (*Sylvio Dokov*)

111

the head but their classmates may not have the benefit of a head protector!

In order to make taekwondo suitable for the under-sixteens, this form of competition should be eliminated. To make training suitable for under-twelves, all high kicks must be taken out of the syllabus. Taekwondo techniques are often tested against wood and bricks. This practice is strictly out for the under eighteens.

Thai Boxing

Thai boxing is full contact minus the padded footguards, so if you didn't care for the latter, then you definitely will not like Thai boxing. Young people are taught to develop forceful impacts delivered by practical techniques (*fig 181*). Light sparring shows how these techniques can be applied in a street situation. Full force sparring causes brain damage!

A National Syllabus

The following remarks exclude judo, kendo and perhaps nippon kempo. Producing a young person's syllabus may well tax the ingenuity of any single martial art so it may be necessary to import training routines

fig 181. Thai boxing is dangerously practical and ripe for misuse in the playground. (*Sylvio Dokov*)

fig 182. This rather effective kick should be changed to a pushing action delivered with the sole of the foot.

from other traditions. The following syllabus has been put together from a selection of the above martial arts. It is designed for the under-twelves and is 'martial arty' without teaching potentially dangerous techniques.

Falling children are taught roll-outs and breakfalls. All roll-outs must conclude in a standing position.

Body movement children are taught the cardinal points of evasion. The attacker lunges forward with an outstretched arm.

Blocking children are taught circular and elbow blocks, using aids such as a light ball and a plastic pipe.

Punching thrusting, not snapping punches are taught from formal stances. These do not stress focus or power and are not pulled back.

Kicking thrusting, not snapping kicks are taught from basic stances. These do not stress focus or power and are not snapped back. Kicks to the head, groin and knees are not taught. The sole of the foot and the instep are used as striking areas (*fig 182*).

Sparring sticking hands, pushing hands and rolling hands are taught. No free sparring is taught. Pre-arranged sparring may also be taught if the techniques are vetted.

113

Throws only those throws using trips and leverage against the body are taught. Judo-type jackets allow the tunic to be gripped, rather than limbs.

Holds the only holds allowed are those which attack the shoulder and elbow. Even then, leverage must be deliberately muted by applying it close to the fulcrum. The essence of these holds is to restrain the opponent, rather than to coerce.

Groundwork groundwork using body weight and approved holds is allowed.

The Training Log

Coaches often have different preferences for techniques and routines. Some enjoy teaching interactive practice, others basic technique, etc. The effect of this preference is often to give it more time than other aspects of training with the result that when a grading examination is due, students have a patchy knowledge of the syllabus requirement. A way around this is to look at each technique and routine in the syllabus and to decide how much time must be allocated in order to reach an acceptable level of skill in it.

If junior gradings occur every six weeks, and training is held twice a week in ninety minute sessions, then the coach has 1,080 minutes to teach the syllabus requirements. Assuming that the attention span of the average under-twelve-year-old student is only five minutes, then the coach has 216 'units' of time. This does not take into account warm-up, cool-down, or body preparation time and only 170 units are probably available both to learn new techniques and to brush-up on old ones. The coach may decide that a front thrusting kick requires 12 units to learn but that sticking hands requires 24 units. In this way he allocates units of training and is quickly able to see how many techniques can be effectively taught to an acceptable standard during the inter-grading period.

Come the grading examination and he can soon see where the median performance lies. If a large proportion of the class is of a low standard in a particular technique, then the coach will have to review the allocation given, perhaps removing units from a technique in which their general standard is overly high. At worst, techniques or routines will have to be shifted to the next grading interval.

It has been suggested that this will rule out the spontaneity that so often lifts an ordinary session into becoming an inspired one. This is not so. If the coach finds that a particular class is enjoying a routine, then he has the flexibility to continue working that vein – so long as the over-ruled units of other techniques are made up later on.

A training log should be completed by the coach, if not by the students too. This records which techniques the class did on which night and how the students enjoyed the session. This is very helpful in showing up weaknesses in performance at grading time. Little Johnnie may complain that he only got a second class pass but reference to his personal training log shows that he missed crucial units, so one or more of his techniques have suffered.

Not all students will learn at the same rate and any programme must make provision for extra 'remedial units' to improve areas of weakness. These can be covered in additional training sessions set aside for the purpose.

Training logs need be no more than a notebook in which students and coach record training details. However, once unit-allocation has been finalised, then printed sheets held together by a plastic spine can be supplied. More professional clubs may offer 'filofax' type inserts in a small plastic file.

Gradings

Gradings came late to martial art practice! Originally you didn't need to have a black belt; all you had to do was to survive on the battlefield! When martial arts changed to leisure-type activities, the idea of a 'ladder of progression' was adopted. At first there were only two grades – trainee or black belt. Next came novice, intermediate grade, high grade and black belt. Now there are between six and nine stages between the adult novice and black belt.

Why were gradings introduced? Gradings represented a tangible reward for effort. Black belt was several years into the future, so what more ready reward was available for hard training? Answer: the coloured belt. Coloured belts represent more easily realisable goals. The adult grades every 12/24 weeks but this may be too long an interval for children. Children see time differently to adults. The world is newer and there are more things to experience, so something that is a week away seems like an eternity. This is why I suggest reducing the grading requirement and bringing down grading intervals for the under-twelves to 6 weeks.

> Grading examinations give everyone a chance to see how well they've done. A black belt is several years away but the next coloured belt is only 6/12 weeks off. Each step takes them closer to the coveted black belt!

If there are eight adult grades between novice and black belt, then there should be sixteen for the younger student. Having said that, coaches will be aware that parents are not made of money, so grading costs should be reduced to at least half of the adult rate. Moreover, there should be no belt-change requirement for each and every junior grade. It is less expensive if adult belt colours are used, perhaps with a sewn-on coloured tab to denote a young person's grade. Thus the young student's equivalent to the white belt adult grade is a white belt junior grade. Above this is the junior white belt/black tab grade. The next adult grade of yellow belt translates into the junior syllabus as yellow, followed by yellow with black tab. And so on.

If the coach doesn't want to lose young students, then he will not enter them for a grading unless confident they will pass. He will have used continuous assessment and even if an external examiner takes the grading, the club coach will be on hand to shore up any bad performances on the day with a report of previous standards displayed. So why have the grading anyway? Since the student entered can't fail, the examination may draw out additional skill and give grounds for awarding a higher pass.

Gradings are very important to the young martial artist, so parents and local dignitaries should be invited. It is unlikely that the Press would send a reporter, though they are always interested in publishing a photo or two. It is important that some young martial artists are not made to feel inferior to others – so everybody succeeds and gets a prize, be it a medal or a certificate.

The Award Scheme

As I mentioned at the beginning of this chapter, being a martial artist involves far more than being able to perform techniques. Qualities such as kindness, politeness and respect for others are cardinal requirements. The question is, how can these virtues be encouraged? The best system uses a reward, such as a merit badge. I would propose three levels of award, gold, silver and bronze. These would be silk thread badges based upon the Martial Arts Commission logo and perhaps a certificate co-signed by the club coach and chairman of the Martial Arts Commission.

These awards should be based upon a community service-type system which allocates points out of ten for various activities. Points would be awarded by a Brownie or Cub pack leader, by the head of a voluntary scheme (e.g. of conservation projects), by the school teacher in respect of diligent application to studies and good behaviour, and by parents in recognition of the student's help and support around the house.

Though a national scheme is only in the consideration stage at present, there is no reason why individual clubs and governing bodies should not, in the interim, set up their own. With some experience of using the scheme, they would be in an ideal position subsequently to advise the Commission.

Competitions

It is certainly true that in a competition involving one hundred young martial artists, one goes home pleased – the other ninety-nine go home unhappy! After watching competitions for years, I am more than ever

convinced that they do far more harm than good! Children who are taught the requirements of the martial art mind are exposed to the screaming, shouting and general bad sportsmanship that sadly nowadays attends virtually all martial art competition. If the coach is in there screaming with the rest, then what value have the principles of martial art practice that he espouses?

Parents are no less culpable and a tournament has not gone by where I failed to see at least one incident of a parent angrily remonstrating with the referee! Therefore under the circumstances, I support the action of some governing bodies in banning the under-sixteens from national competition. It would be a good thing if this ban extended into individual schools, where currently children as young as eight compete.

Competitions for the under-twelves should be replaced by national training courses at which merit awards are presented (*fig 183*).

Glossary

Aikido (Jap) 'The way of spirit/harmony' is a Japanese martial art way which uses the opponent's own force to defeat him. Aikido uses mainly grappling techniques and body evasions. Coaches must avoid over-working young wrists, since this may cause permanent damage.

Aiki jutsu (Jap) 'The art of spirit/harmony' is the predecessor of aikido and a school of jiu jitsu. Unless much modified, this is not suitable for teaching to young people.

Armlock A method of applying controlled leverage to the joints of the opponent's arm, so as to restrain him. Armlocks must be taught so the applied leverage is only barely sufficient to hold the opponent immobile.

Arnis de mano (Phil) 'Usage of hand', a Philippino fighting art using the stick, knife and the empty hand. It is totally unsuitable for teaching to young martial artists.

Attention stance Any one of several formal stances used by martial arts students prior to their beginning training. Used as part of discipline games.

Axe kick The foot is swung high into the air and the heel is then dropped onto the opponent's head or collar bones. This technique cannot be controlled and must not be taught to children!

Back fist A punch which uses the back of the knuckles to attack the side of the head or body. The adult version uses a fast, snapping action that is quite unsuitable for young martial artists. The detuned version uses a light unfocused swing.

Back kick A pushing kick performed with the back turned towards the target. The amended kick impacts with the sole of the foot rather than the adult's heel.

Ball of foot The pad of flesh on the bottom of the foot exposed when the toes are drawn back. Not used when teaching young children.

Basics These are the elementary techniques of a martial art, upon which all else is built. The manner of teaching these may need some alteration to make them suitable for use by younger martial artists.

Belt A strip of coloured fabric worn around the waist, the colour of which denotes the wearer's achievement. Additional children's grades should be identified by means of a sewn-on tab.

Bersilat (Mal) 'To fight', a Malaysian martial art system of armed and unarmed combat. Not enough is known about the way this minority martial art is taught in Britain to make it feasible to offer any comments.

Black belt Signifies that the wearer has attained an understanding of a martial art. The extent of that understanding varies in accordance with the grade of black belt held.

Blocking Use of the body, arm or leg to interrupt or divert an attack. Blocking games improve effectiveness.

Bow To incline the body and head as a mark of respect. It is part of the courtesy ritual which the sensible coach uses to inculcate feelings of respect towards oneself and others.

Breakfall A way of landing safely after falling. This is an essential part of training for the young martial artist, though kendo students may be exempted.

Breaking A method of impact power testing with the body's natural weapons. It is strictly forbidden to all martial artists below the age of eighteen.

Buddhism A Far Eastern religio-philosophy which has had a major effect on the practice of the martial arts through its emphasis upon self-discipline and its rejection of the notion of a permanent soul. Only shorinji kempo teaches Buddhist principles and concerned parents should raise this issue with the coach.

Budo (Jap) 'Martial way'. A method of practising the martial arts so as to improve one's character. Regrettably nowadays, the principles are little understood and almost never applied.

Bujutsu (Jap) 'Martial art', the fighting arts used by Japanese warriors. These are unsuitable for teaching to youngsters.

Butterfly knife Short, broad bladed knife used in pairs for kung fu practice. Their usage must not be taught to children.

Centre of gravity A point in the body around which weight is evenly balanced. It is situated approximately at navel height. Leverage applied across the centre of gravity is the principle of many suitable throws.

Chi sao (Chi) 'Sticking hands', a method of training in kung fu which teaches sensitivity to the opponent's actions. This has excellent potential for the young martial artist as long as it is detuned and taught without the jolting strikes.

Choke A grappling technique which stops the opponent from breathing. This should not be taught!

Circular block Any deflection technique which moves in a circle. Many games can be built around circular blocks.

Claw hand Open hand technique in which the fingers hook. Not recommended for children's usage.

Combination technique When two or more basic techniques are linked together into a sequence.

Control Regulation of force used during blows and kicks. This is an essential element of all practice.

Coordination Moving the body and limbs to the correct extent and in the correct sequence. Good training builds coordination.

Crane One of the animals used as a model for schools of kung fu. It uses large light movements which children enjoy, though the eye attacks must be omitted.

Crescent kick A circular kick that sweeps the sole of the vertical foot across the front of the body. A suitable kick for children to learn.

Dan (Jap) 'Rank', a stage of proficiency within the black belt and sometimes indicated by yellow or gold stripes. Young children can become black belts though this does not necessarily make them martial artists!

Dojang (Kor) 'Place of training' for martial art practice.

Dojo (Jap) 'Place of training in the way', the traditional training hall in which martial art principles are taught together with technique.

Escrima (Phil) Another name for Arnis de mano.

External system Any Chinese fighting system which stresses the importance of muscular power. External systems must be detuned before they can be taught to children.

Flying kick Any kick which is delivered when both feet are clear of the floor. Children enjoy performing these but the target should never be above chest height.

Focus Most impact techniques are aimed at a specific target and delivered so as to develop maximum impact there. The concentration of impact force is 'focus'. This concept must not be taught to children.

Forearm block Any deflection technique which uses that portion of the arm between the wrist and the elbow. Use interactive games to teach advanced principles and to build coordination.

Forward stance A basic stance in which the hips are turned to face the front, the front knee is bent and the rear knee is straightened. This is the stance most used by young martial artists during punch and kick delivery.

Freestyle sparring Most advanced form of sparring in which unprogrammed techniques are exchanged. Except for practitioners of kendo and judo, children below the age of twelve should not be allowed to participate.

Front kick Kick in which the knee rises to the front and the kick is thrust smoothly out. The sole of the foot is used to deliver the junior version.

Full contact A fighting system in which full power techniques are used to knock the opponent out. It is definitely not suitable for children to practise!

Goju ryu (Jap) 'Hard/soft tradition', a style of karate based upon shorei ryu and founded by Kannryo Higaonna. Children should be exempted from ancillary weight training and from rigorous performance of sanchin kata.

Goshin jutsu (Jap) 'Self defence art', practical techniques of self defence. These are quite impractical for young people.

Grappling techniques Fighting systems which use locks, holds and throws to defeat the opponent. These are better for the younger martial artists than unmodified impact based alternatives.

Groundwork Judo techniques applied when both parties are on the ground. Children enjoy the rough and tumble of groundwork.

Guard The way in which the body, arms and legs are arranged, allowing maximum potential usage of body weapons whilst reducing target opportunities for the opponent.

Hammer fist A blow with the little-finger edge of the fist. This does not damage the knuckles and should be taught with a loose circular action.

Hapkido (Kor) 'Way of spirit/body harmony', the Korean equivalent of aikido, though it also includes a wide variety of striking techniques. From the point of view of training children, this shares the disadvantages of both aikido and karate.

Heel kick Any kick which uses the heel to strike the opponent. The sole of the foot version should be taught to children.

Hold An immobilising technique capable of holding a person without necessarily hurting him.

Hold down A technique applied during groundwork to immobilise the opponent and prevent him from rising.

Horse stance The feet are wide apart and the knees bend equally. The back is straight.

Hsing-I (Chi) Form of kung fu which does not use great muscular power and which relies upon linear movements. It is suitable for teaching to children.

Hung gar (Chi) A prominent style of southern shaolin kung fu, believed to be an ancestor of karate. This must be detuned when taught to children.

Iaido (Jap) 'Way of the sword', the drawing, using and returning of the Japanese sword. Young children would not only find it impossible to wield a sword, they would find the philosophy incomprehensible.

Iai jutsu (Jap) 'Sword art', the practical tradition of drawing, cutting with and re-sheathing the sword. See above comments.

Ibuki (Jap) 'Breath control', a method of breathing in which air is noisily forced out. Children find this hilarious, though it often causes sore throats.

Inner block Block in which the forearm sweeps from the outside of the body to the inside. Taught as part of interactive games.

Internal system A system of kung fu in which power is not generated by obvious muscular action. All of these systems are suitable for young people.

Jiu jitsu (Jap) 'Compliant art', a system of grappling which avoids meeting force with force. Unfortunately it does include techniques which are quite unsuitable for young children.

Jiu kumite (Jap) 'Free sparring', where techniques can be exchanged but a measure of control is retained. Children under twelve should not free spar.

Judo (Jap) 'Compliant way', a school of jiu jitsu refined by the late Jigoro Kano into an Olympic combat sport. This is probably the best martial art for young children.

Karate (Jap) 'Empty hand', an Okinawan fighting system transported to Japan where it was refined into a martial way. Considerable modification of the syllabus is required before it can be taught to children.

Karate do (Jap) 'The way of karate', a study of karate for sporting or character-building reasons. Same comments apply as above.

Kendo (Jap) 'Way of the sword', a combat sport which uses armour and the bamboo shinai. The equipment is expensive to buy and children all too soon grow out of it. For youngsters whose parents who can afford it, kendo is great fun and quite safe.

Kiai (Jap) 'Spirit harmony', the joining of the will to body action and expressed as a loud shout. Children enjoy shouting!

Kick boxing Another name for full contact. Avoid!

Kobudo (Jap) 'Old martial way', a term used to describe the practice of classical budo systems. Not applicable to children.

Kohai (Jap) Class junior.

Krabee krabong (Tha) Thai fighting system using a pair of short swords, or a short sword and a shield. Quite unsuitable for children.

Kung fu (Chi) The common name applied to schools of Chinese martial art practised outside of the Chinese mainland. External schools must be modified, internal schools can be taught as they are.

Kyokushinkai (Jap) 'Way of ultimate truth association', the name of a karate school founded by the Korean, Masutatsu Oyama. Unsuitable for teaching to children without considerable modification.

Kyudo (Jap) 'Way of the bow'. A martial way based upon kyu jutsu. Incomprehensible to most children.

Lock The name given to a technique that immobilises a joint by applying leverage across it. Children's locks must reduce the degree of leverage until it is just sufficient to hold the opponent immobile.

Long hand boxing Any school of Chinese martial art which uses punches relying on full elbow extension. Medicine balls can be used to train for powerful thrusting actions but care must be taken not to extend the elbows fully.

Lunge punch An advancing punch normally delivered from a forward stance. This is one of the basic techniques of karate and the children's version must omit focus and power, substituting a smooth, thrusting action instead.

Makiwara (Jap) 'Straw padded post', a training aid for the fist. It must not be used by the under-eighteens.

Martial arts Military techniques, or those techniques used by the classical warrior. It is unlikely that any child could aspire to the title 'martial artist' though he could attain black belt.

Mokuso (Jap) 'Quiet thought', a pause for meditation. Often used after training to ready children for return to normal life.

Muay Thai (Tha) Thai boxing, a form of full contact, using boxing gloves and developed in Thailand. Quite unsuitable for persons under sixteen years of age.

Ninjutsu (Jap) 'The techniques of stealing in'. No longer taught and quite unsuitable for children even if still available.

Nippon kempo (Jap) 'Japanese boxing', which uses a kendo type protective helmet, breastplate and boxing gloves. Provided powerful punches/kicks are not taught, children can enjoy this!

Northern styles A family of kung fu systems characterised by large movements and lots of kicks. Children love the expansive, sweeping movements but head kicks should not be taught.

Nunchaku (Jap) 'Wooden flail' made from two wooden batons linked by a chain or thong. Many youngsters are prosecuted each year for possession of rice flails. Their use must not be taught to children.

One knuckle fist Fist in which the middle joint of the index or middle finger leads the others. Not suitable for children because they end up hurting their knuckles.

One step sparring Training system in which the attacker performs a single, pre-arranged attack and the defender responds in an agreed manner. Provided the attack and defence are carefully chosen, this should provide children with a useful interactive training aid.

Outside block A forearm block which sweeps from the inside to the outside of the body. Teach as an interactive game against a plastic pipe or soft ball.

Pak mei 'White eyebrows', a style of kung fu named after the originator's nickname. Spasm actions used in punches and full elbow extensions make this style unsuitable for children unless modified.

Pa kua 'Eight trigrams', one of the three internal schools of kung fu. The movements are soft and suitable for children to learn. Eye strikes must be omitted, however.

Palmheel Thrusting strike with the heel of the hand. Taught as a push.

Parry To deflect a blow or kick. Children are taught not to meet force with force.

Peh hoke (Chi) 'White crane', style of kung fu characterised by evasion and counter-attack. Children love the large movements but eye-strikes must not be taught.

Penjak silat (Indo) The national martial art of Indonesia, using both armed and unarmed combat. Unsuitable for children.

Praying mantis Style of kung fu characterised by strong arm movements and powerful muscle spasm. Must be detuned and softened before it can be taught to children.

Pre-arranged sparring Pair-form sparring in which both the attack and defence are known beforehand. Provided both are carefully selected by the coach, this becomes a valid alternative to free sparring.

Randori (Jap) 'Free exercise', the name for free sparring in judo. It is one of the few forms of free sparring suitable for children.

Reap Taking the opponent's supporting leg away. A term used in judo for a variety of safe throws.

Reverse punch A punch delivered with the opposite fist to the leading leg. A foam ball is an excellent training aid because it helps produce a smooth, thrusting movement.

Reverse roundhouse kick A kick delivered with the sole of the foot travelling in a horizontal arc and striking no higher than chest height.

Ridge hand A circular strike using the thumb-side of the hand edge. Usually used against groin or throat, so it should not be taught to children.

Roundhouse kick A kick delivered with the instep travelling in a horizontal arc. Not to be taught above chest height.

Roundhouse punch A punch that travels along a circular path, using a relaxed throwing action.

Ryu (Jap) 'Tradition', the core of teachings which separate one school from another.

Sabom (Kor) 'Teacher'.

Sacrifice throws Judo throws in which one is prepared to fall in the process of throwing the opponent. Suitable for older children.

Sai (Jap) A short handled and heavy trident which can serve also as a truncheon. Like all martial arts using weapons, this should not be taught to children.

Sempai (Jap) 'Senior', the next senior grade in the training hall below the instructor.

Sensei (Jap) 'Teacher'.

Shaolin (Chi) Famous Buddhist monastery associated with martial art practice. It is still in existence (in a rebuilt form) today.

Shito ryu (Jap) School of karate founded by Kenwa Mabuni. Must be amended before children can practise.

Shorinji kempo (Jap) 'Shaolin Temple Boxing', a Japanese rendering of shaolin kung fu. Sometimes involves indoctrination in Buddhist teachings.

Shotokan (Jap) 'Shoto's club', the name given to Gichin Funakoshi's Japanese honbu. It is also used to describe a style of karate which can, after modification, be taught to children.

Shukokai (Jap) 'Way for all', an offshoot of Mabuni's shito ryu founded by the latter's student, Chojiro Tani. Would need major alteration to make it suitable for children.

Shuriken (Jap) Sharp edged throwing star. Possession of one is a criminal offence.

Side kick A kick using the heel and edge of the foot and driven out while the body is turned sideways-on to the opponent. Modify to pushing impact with the sole of the foot.

Sifu (Chi) 'Teacher'.

Silat (Indo) 'Fast action', a general term for Indonesian martial arts; some armed, some unarmed and all unsuitable for children.

Snap kick Any kick that is smartly retrieved after use. The retrieval action depends upon muscle elasticity. Snap kicking injures joints and must not be taught to children.

Southern styles Collective name given for schools of kung fu characterised by strong stances and few kicks. Most of these use strong spasm action of muscles and full elbow extension − both of which are unsuitable for children to learn.

Sparring The exchange of techniques with a partner. These techniques may be agreed beforehand, or be completely free. With the sole exceptions of judo and kendo, free sparring is not advised for children.

Spear hand Hand weapon which thrusts the extended fingers into the target. Not to be taught to children.

Staff A wooden pole about six feet long. Too heavy for a child to use.

Stamping kick One which drives the heel downward into the target. Stamping kicks must not be taught to children.

Stance The way in which body weight is poised and stable.

Sticking hands Form of sparring practice in Wing Chun kung fu, which relies upon feeling the opponent's intent and responding. Excellent basis for children's practice.

Style A particular rendering of a martial way or martial art based upon an individual interpretation.

Sweep The opponent's supporting foot is displaced by a hook or strike, so he loses balance. Children can use the hook action safely.

Taekwondo (Kor) 'Kick/punch way', an umbrella term for the martial arts of Korea though it is now developing a single, common identity. Breaking techniques, snap kicks, head kicks and focus must all be excluded from children's practice.

Tai chi chuan (Chi) Cantonese reading of 'Great ultimate fist', one of the three internal Chinese martial arts. Quite suitable for children, especially when performed quickly.

Tang soo do (Kor) 'Way of the Tang hand', a fighting system strongly influenced by karate but now pursuing its own line of development. Must be detuned as for taekwondo if taught to children.

Thai boxing See 'Muay Thai'.

Tonfa (Jap) 'Handle', an Okinawan covert weapon used in karate practice. Not to be taught to children.

Uechi ryu (Jap) A style of Okinawan karate founded by Kanbun Uechi. Children will not understand sanchin and must not be taught to use the big toe for front kicks.

Upward block Any deflection technique that travels upwards. Use plastic pipe or a foam ball to develop effectiveness.

Wado ryu (Jap) 'Way of harmony tradition', a karate style founded by Hironori Ohtsuka. Must be amended before children can practise it. Particularly damaging to the knee joints.

Wing chun (Chi) Style of southern kung fu devised by the Buddhist nun Ng Mui. Rather too effective for comfort, though children would otherwise enjoy the 'rolling hands' routine.

Wu shu (Chi) 'Martial art', umbrella term to describe the martial arts of the Chinese mainland. 'Kung fu à gogo' – great fun and suitable for children of all ages.

X-block Where the forearms cross over to stop the attacking technique from reaching its target. Teach using a plastic pipe.

Zen (Jap) A Buddhist sect often associated with martial art practice.

Index

aerobic training 14–15, 37
aeroplane 26, 86
agility 19, 40, 41, 62
agility games 39–42
aikido 10, 107, 118
anaerobic training 15, 19, 37
ankle pull 25
award scheme 116

black belt 9, 92, 101, 105, 106, 115, 119
blocks 65–80, 113, 119, 120, 121, 124, 127
body evasion games 62, 64
body lifts 32, 33
boxing 107, 110
breakfall 59–60, 61, 113, 119
bridge 25, 54, 98, 99
bridging games 53–54
British Judo Association 11

Canney, Dr J.C. 7, 14, 16, 18
canoe 32, 34
Code of Conduct 11, 13, 101
competition 9, 17, 18, 19, 116–117
crawl-over 36

donkey 28, 29
duty of care 9, 10

fall guy 42, 43
falls 58, 113
fitness 14–16, 19
flexibility training 15–16, 19, 34, 52
focus 81, 82, 113, 120
formal training 66, 71, 72, 80, 83
full contact 107, 110, 121

grading 17, 18, 102, 114, 115–116
grappling-based martial arts 21, 27, 44,
    58, 102, 103, 107, 121
groundwork 53, 98, 114, 121
Gummerson, Tony 7, 15

hapkido 10, 107
hold-down 54, 98, 100, 122
holds 100, 114, 122
hyper-extension 26

impact-based martial arts 27, 48, 102, 103
injury 10, 11, 13, 16, 102
insurance 10, 11, 102
interactive training 66, 74

jiu jitsu 10, 44, 103, 107, 111, 122
judo 9, 44, 103, 107–108, 112, 114, 122
jumps 27, 39, 40, 42

karate 9, 10, 22, 105, 108–109, 111, 122
kendo 58, 109–110, 112, 123
kicks 10, 16, 25, 26, 40, 65, 69, 83, 85, 86,
    88, 113, 114, 120, 121, 125, 126
kinaesthetic awareness games 22–24
kung fu 9, 10, 74, 88, 110, 123

leapfrog and tunnel 39
licence 11, 102
lifting the log 32, 42, 43

Martial Arts Commission (MAC) 9, 11, 12,
    14, 101, 102, 103, 116
mounted wrestling 46

ninjutsu 110, 124
nippon kempo 110, 112, 124

physically disadvantaged children
    103–104
pull-back 82, 83
punches 10, 48, 49, 65, 69, 74, 81–83,
    113, 125
push-overs 62, 64
pushing hands 104, 110, 113

rollalong 21

rolling hands 92, 93, 113
roll-outs 21, 59, 113

scrum 44
shape games 25–26
shorinji kempo 10, 111
sparring 12, 13, 18, 113, 121, 124, 125,
    126
spatial awareness games 21, 27
stances 22–24, 48, 65, 70, 81, 85, 86, 88,
    113, 121, 126
standing position 57, 113
sticking hands 88–93, 113, 114, 126
strength games 27–32, 42–51
stress 17–18
Superman exercise 26
suppleness games 32–37
syllabus 9, 11, 17, 25, 101, 102, 103,
    105–117

taekwondo 9, 10, 22, 103, 111, 126–127
tai chi chuan 91, 104, 127
technique progression 58, 59, 81
Thai boxing 112, 127
throws 10, 32, 42, 52, 94–98, 114, 125
thrust 33, 42, 48, 56, 86, 90, 91, 92, 93,
    113
timing 40, 41, 62, 63, 80, 83
train 82
training facilities 10–11
training log 114–115
tug of war 44, 45
tugalong 28, 30, 31
twister 46

warm-down 37, 38
warm-up 20–37, 38, 58
wheelbarrows 27–28
White, John 7, 26
wing chun kung fu 103, 127
wu shu 110, 127